confirm, expand, and apply Moltmann's solid theology to their particular areas of expertise.

M. DOUGLAS MEEKS shows how Moltmann's thought results in a fresh approach to practical theology.

RODNEY J. HUNTER relates pastoral care and counseling to Moltmann's theology of hope and calls for a more biblically based perspective involving the entire body of the local church.

JAMES W. FOWLER relates church education to Moltmann's theology. He suggests that Christian education ought to be education for creative discipleship in the context of the coming kingdom of God.

NOEL L. ERSKINE points to parallels between Moltmann's theology and black theology, and points to some critical differences.

The concluding chapter is a response by Dr. Moltmann to his discussion partners' interpretations.

Encouraging and yet challenging, this book demonstrates how the message of the kingdom of God affects the way all Christians are called to minister in the world. In a time when discouragement seems the order of the day, this intriguing study offers good news for laity and clergy as it brings help and hope for the future of the church.

THE AUTHORS

JÜRGEN MOLTMANN is professor of systematic theology at the University of Tübingen in Germany. He has served on major committees of the World Alliance of Reformed Churches and many of his works are available in English.

M. DOUGLAS MEEKS is professor of theology and ethics at Eden Theological Seminary in Oklahoma.

RODNEY J. HUNTER is associate professor of pastoral theology at the Candler School of Theology.

JAMES W. FOWLER is associate professor of theology and human development at Candler School of Theology.

NOEL L. ERSKINE is assistant professor of theology and ethics at Candler School of Theology.

THEODORE RUNYON is professor of systematic theology at Candler School of Theology.

Hope for the Church

Hope

ABINGDON • Nashville

JÜRGEN MOLTMANN

with
M. Douglas Meeks

Rodney J. Hunter

James W. Fowler

Noel L. Erskine

Edited and translated by
Theodore Runyon

for the Church

Moltmann in Dialogue with Practical Theology

Hope for the Church:
Moltmann in Dialogue with Practical Theology

Copyright © 1979 by Abingdon

Library of Congress Cataloging in Publication Data

MOLTMANN, JÜRGEN.
   Hope for the church.
   1. Moltmann, Jürgen—Addresses, essays, lectures.   2.   Hope—Addresses, essays, lectures.   3.   Theology, Practical—Addresses, essays,
lectures.   I.   Meeks, M. Douglas.   II.   Runyon, Theodore.   III.   Title.
BX4827.M6A53   230′.092′4   79-14732

ISBN 0-687-17360-4

Scripture quotations unless otherwise noted are from the Revised Standard
Version of the Bible, copyrighted 1946, 1952, © 1971, 1973 by the Division
of Christian Education of the National Council of Churches of Christ in the
U.S.A.

MANUFACTURED BY THE PARTHENON PRESS AT
NASHVILLE, TENNESSEE, UNITED STATES OF AMERICA

Preface

The chapters of this book, which probe the implications of Jürgen Moltmann's thought for the various disciplines of practical theology, were originally delivered as a lecture series, "A Theology of Hope and Parish Practice," at the 1978 Ministers' Week sponsored by Emory University's Candler School of Theology. The enthusiastic response of the participants at that conference indicated a genuine hunger on the part of many pastors and laypersons for resources that apply solid theological thinking to the practical life of the church. This book now makes those lectures, in revised form, available to a wider audience.

Professor Moltmann's own warmth, openness, and willingness to enter into lively dialogue, as well as his profound concern for the life of the church everywhere, can be felt on every page of his chapters. And the challenge of his thought calls forth from each of his discussion partners a serious joint effort to demonstrate how the message of the kingdom of God affects the way in which all Christians are called to minister in the world.

The original lectures were made possible by the following lectureships of the Candler School of Theology: the Quillian Lectureship, the Sam P. Jones Lectureship, the William Wallace Duncan Lectureship and the A. J. and C. C. Jarrell Lectureship.

Theodore Runyon
Emory University

Contents

Introduction
Theodore Runyon

In the English-speaking world, the name of Tübingen theologian Jürgen Moltmann is primarily associated with his first major work, *Theology of Hope.*[1] That book established Moltmann as the leading spokesman of a highly influential movement in contemporary religious thought, one which has had to be taken into account by every theologian writing during the past decade. Liberation theologies, third-world theologies, even the "theology of play," show the effects of his eschatological interpretation of the Christian faith. The depth and richness of Moltmann's position have further come to light with the appearance of the second and third volumes of his dogmatics, *The Crucified God*[2] and *The Church in the Power of the Spirit.*[3] These make the full range of his trinitarian thinking available and allow for the kind of encounter that can open up the implications of his thought in all directions.

The present book is the first to bring Moltmann into direct dialogue with theologians representing the traditional practical disciplines of pastoral care, preaching, religious education, and Christian social witness. According to Moltmann, good theology must be *practical* theology. He addresses the problems of ministry not just because of his own years of pastoral experience, but because practice is at the heart of his theological method. Theology is the theory of the future of the church, and its purpose is to make a difference in the shape of that future. To be sure, theology has often been turned in other directions and been employed for other purposes. It has been preoccupied with past doctrines and dogmas that seemed of little import to the current life of the church or the world. It has also served to rationalize the way things are, and to defend established beliefs and practices against any who would question them. Theology's primary task is neither to preserve nor to defend, but to be the discipline by which the church tests its present reality in the light of its vocation as the herald of the new future of God.

From Moltmann's standpoint, the distinctive contribution of Christian faith is the hope it engenders in the midst of the ambiguous and even hopeless circumstances that plague human existence. The gospel makes the inexhaustible resources of the kingdom of God available to the believing individual and the faithful church. A practical theology that operates out of an eschatological context is able to view things not just as they have been, or even as they are, but in terms of their possibilities and potential.[4] But is not such an approach, that refuses to settle for reality as it now is, "unrealistic"? To the contrary, insists Moltmann, to settle for what is now "real" is to be tied to what is passing away and soon will be no more. Far from being unrealistic, a *hopeful* approach "alone takes seriously the possibilities with which all reality is fraught. It does not take things as they happen to stand or lie, but as progressing, moving things with possibilities of change."[5] In hope lies the "greater realism" because it enables us to cooperate with those tendencies which can become actual if nurtured and cultivated. What is hope today is reality tomorrow—if hope elicits planning and sacrifice on the part of a committed community. Thus the church that lives in terms of the kingdom is involved in transformation. It is in "the conversion business," says Roman Catholic theologian Bernard Lonergan, and can never be satisfied with things as they are. This dedication to change endures—"until He comes!"

The implications of this for preaching, pastoral counseling, religious education, and Christian social concerns are far reaching, as a leading American authority on Moltmann, **Douglas Meeks,** points out. *Preaching* that understands itself to be happening within an eschatological context is an extension of God's own creative power that raised Jesus from the dead and ushered in the new age in him. For Moltmann, preaching is "*pro*-clamation" and "*pro*-nouncement," offering a future which is *for* human beings because it is an alternative to the forces of death, oppression, and destruction that threaten existence on every hand. "The risen Christ calls, sends, justifies, and sanctifies men, and in so doing gathers, calls, and sends them into his eschatological future for the world."[6] The faith which the preaching of God's new future makes possible sees beyond the frustrations and defeats of the present. It is characterized by patience, which is the willingness to endure waiting and even suffering in the confidence that God's sovereignty will finally triumph. "Patience is the greatest art of those who hope. Hope accepts the 'cross of the present' in the 'power of the resurrection.' It takes upon itself the real unredeemed state of the present as it is, the torture and the pain of the negative, without resignation and without illusion."[7] Thus the preached word that takes its inspiration from the coming kingdom is a word that proclaims the cross as well as the resurrection—the cross as seen through the resurrection, and the resurrection as seen through the cross. Moreover, Meeks claims that for Moltmann preaching is adequate only as it is consciously *trinitarian:* the cross of the Son is the means used by the Father to bring new, reconciled life out of death and create a community that shares in the gifts of the Spirit for celebration and service, anticipating the age to come.

Pastoral care and counseling are also affected by this turn to the future as the source out of which the practical life of the church is to be understood, asserts pastoral psychologist **Rodney J. Hunter.** The Freudian models of therapy, which have been of major influence in pastoral care, understand the person primarily as the product of his or her past conditioning. Therapy involves a long and time-consuming process of bringing these causal factors to the surface and to consciousness. Without denying the legitimacy of this approach, one who is charged with the care of souls in an average-size congregation has neither the expertise nor the sheer time required to carry out such counseling competently. Without access to expensive referral services, the pastor is at a loss to know how to assist those who need release from the events and relations of the past in which they are imprisoned. The announcement of the kingdom on the lips of Jesus never glosses over or denies the depth of human sin and degradation. Obviously the harlot and the tax collector were conditioned by years of public rejection, recrimination, and shame, as well as by deep-seated religious guilt. The announcement of the kingdom comes first to them as an indication of the radicality of the break with the past which the redeemed future offers. Healing is made possible on the new foundation that is none other than Christ and his cross, God's radical affirmation of the sinner as the object of his reconciling care. When one is gripped by the ultimacy of this new foundation and the possibilities it opens up, one does not straightway forget the past as if it had no continuing importance or influence. Yet one is released from bondage to the vicious cycles of the past and is given new conditions under which the past can be sorted out and dealt with in the confidence that one's destiny is not determined solely by what has been, but is to be found in Christ and his lordship. If the basic battle has been won, the mopping up operations, though not without pain and their own dangers, are conducted in a different frame of mind than if the battle itself were still in doubt.

Christian therapists need not hide their light under a bushel, claims Hunter, because pastoral counseling can operate out of decidedly theological perspectives and should not labor under the impression that not only its techniques but also its basic theoretical models must come from secular sources. There has been confusion precisely at this point according to Hunter and Meeks. Preoccupied with winning acceptance in psychotherapeutic circles, pastoral counseling has tended to adopt uncritically the values of, and draw its basic metaphors from, the world of its secular counterparts. The result is a crisis in identity: a discipline practiced under church auspices finds itself hard put to say how it differs significantly from therapy in a non-Christian context.

What are the distinctive features lent by a Christian perspective? Are the biblical definitions of sickness and health, and the goals of human existence, the same as those dictated by contemporary secular society? Using a case study, Hunter demonstrates how insights from *Theology of Hope* and *The Crucified God* can change the way we do pastoral care. For Moltmann, *Christian education* is closely related to the theology of baptism. It is the nurturing process that takes place prior to baptism and the continuing reflection on the meaning and implications of Christian discipleship to which baptism commits us. **James W. Fowler** shows how important the creative imagination is in this process and finds in Moltmann's eschatological orientation the theological underpinnings for a theory of the Christian imagination.

Traditionally, the task of religious education has been to indoctrinate each new generation in the heritage, lore, and wisdom of the past. Thus it has often been backward-looking, preoccupied with the perpetuation and cultivation of values from previous generations. Such an approach is endemically conservative and tends to reinforce the religious and cultural status quo—*unless* what is recalled from the past is a prophetic vision of a new future. The goal of Christian education can be nothing less than "the kingdom of God and his righteousness." It should be, therefore, a continuously creative and innovative force within the church's life, for the promises of the kingdom can never be completely fulfilled by any structure or program that we by our ingenuity and hard work might accomplish. Though Moltmann is occasionally accused of reintroducing the once-popular liberal notion of "building the kingdom," it should be evident that his eschatological theology is not to be confused with that progressivist and incremental understanding sometimes associated (wrongly!) with the name of Walter Rauschenbusch. For Moltmann the kingdom is always on the horizon, never within our grasp. It exercises a constant critique over against all partial realizations of which we are capable. At the same time, the kingdom is *not* a "counsel of despair"—the function that some of Reinhold Niebuhr's detractors felt the kingdom played in his thought: an infinitely regressing absolute that so thoroughly relativizes every human achievement as to make moral distinctions meaningless. Such a position would see every alternative as equidistant from the kingdom and every attempt at reform as carrying within it the same prideful seeds of destruction found in the present order. Thus any alternative to the present state of affairs would be regarded as equally unpromising with the result that the status quo, miserable as it may be, becomes, if not the best of all possible worlds, at least no worse than the other options. Such a view is tantamount, says Moltmann, to a "utopia of the status quo."

Rejecting both evolutionary optimism and pessimistic "realism," Moltmann regards the kingdom proclaimed by Jesus, not only as the source of critical principles by which to judge the inadequacies of the present, but the source of the creative vision of "a city whose builder and maker is God" which, by the power of the Spirit, can shape and affect present history positively. Thus Moltmann demarcates himself from the student anarchists of the 60s, who practiced negation for its own sake, and from certain tendencies he observes in those Latin American theologians of liberation who, in their antagonism toward western capitalism and the ills it has visited upon their countries, seem too willing to sacrifice the hard-won benefits of democracy in favor of the facile promises of totalitarian solutions. The vision of the kingdom as the source of new possibilities for the future implies a judicious and responsible weighing of alternatives in an effort to find the optimum response at this juncture in time in the light of Jesus' disclosure of the nature of his Father's reign.

This is why the religious imagination, the theme Fowler pursues in his chapter, plays such an important role in creative discipleship. And it is the reason Christian education must counteract the deadening, dulling, drugging effect which secular culture has on the imaginations of children and adults alike. Secular culture narrows vision and reduces options to "more of the same"—camouflaged of course in packages labeled "new" and "better" to disguise their essential bankruptcy. In such a milieu, a religious education that trains the imagination to see alternatives to cultural mediocrity is an exercise not only in discipleship but in citizenship as well. The sources for democratic renewal lie with those who, in their vision of what God intends for humankind, cannot wait for heaven but seek to implement here and now the first fruits of the kingdom that already are possible through the power and gifts of the Spirit.

It is this kind of impatience with things as they are and a conviction that, in the light of God's promises, they can be different which informs black theology and the life of many black churches in America today. **Noel L. Erskine** sees, therefore, a genuine congruity between the concerns of black theology and Moltmann, who was one of the first on the European scene to take note of black theology and introduce it to European readers. When Moltmann focused attention on hope, he was also forced to take seriously those forces that oppose hope. His work with the World Council of Churches early made him aware of the cruciality of the issue of oppression for third-world Christians, and that issue became a matter of first priority for him, as reflected in his *Religion, Revolution and the Future*,[8] and *The Experiment Hope*.[9] His Christology, *The Crucified God*, also reflects the depth and extent to which this struggle shaped his basic theological position.

Erskine suggests an important difference, however, between an eschatological theology rooted in Moltmann's Calvinist sources and one which arises from the black experience. The Calvinist position, hammered out in conflict with both Lutherans and enthusiasts, insisted that the full reality of God is only a future experience and not of the present. This position was maintained against the Lutheran emphasis on the bodily presence of Christ in the sacrament and against the claims of the enthusiasts that the new age of fulfillment in the Spirit had already arrived. Though Moltmann wants to do justice to the concerns of Luther and the enthusiasts, he opts for the Calvinist position. God's reality in its fullness is a future experience; in the present we have him only under the forms of faith and hope. Moltmann maintains this position in *The Church in the Power of the Spirit*,[10] the third volume of his dogmatics, where the Spirit's power is described as the dialectic between the inexhaustible remembrance of Christ's death and resurrection, on the one hand, and the future kingdom, on the other, in which the divine sovereignty visible to faith and proleptically present in the resurrection will publicly triumph over all evil.

The black church is closer to the enthusiasts. The confidence of black people in the final triumph of God and his righteousness is based not so much on divine promises made in the past, important as these are, or yearnings prompted by the persistence of injustice in the present, but on the palpable experience of God's overwhelming spiritual power. Simply put, if the Spirit is the downpayment (II Cor. 5:5) on that which is to come, the amount of that downpayment is larger in the black church. There is no need for the delayed gratification for which Calvinism is famous. However, present visions of fulfillment do not lessen the demand for change. Indeed, the Spirit is the energizing power for change, providing a taste of the new order. Moreover, the Spirit grants staying power in the midst of frustration, a staying power that other liberationist movements often appear to lack.

The questions which Erskine's chapter raises may be only partially justified. There is every indication that Moltmann, in his doctrine of the Spirit, is attempting to do justice to the power of the Spirit in the Christian life as he has observed that power among black people, third-world churches, and in Eastern Orthodoxy. But Moltmann is concerned lest present fulfillment, either through spiritual experience or sacramentalism, detract from the essentially futuristic orientation that he is convinced is most genuinely biblical. This is a point at which the theology of hope needs to take seriously the fact that the past-present-future time scheme which it takes for granted is much less clearly demarcated in non-western cultures where past and future are more likely to be viewed as extensions of the present and spiritually simultaneous with it. One might ask, moreover, which is closer to the biblical sense of time, western time-consciousness—produced by the Enlightenment, rationalistic historiography and technology—or the third world's spiritual simultaneity?

Erskine's chapter demonstrates the practical difference made in the lives of oppressed peoples by having an alternative world. They do not have to accept reality as defined by the oppressors but can appeal to a transcendent authority who is their confidence. It is God who enables them to maintain their sanity—i.e., their consciousness that life makes sense even when it doesn't. It is God who will not let them deny their own dignity and worth when, reduced to the stark reality of their present circumstances, they might be demoralized and lose hope. And this, after all, is what the creative power of the eschaton, and therefore of eschatological theology, is essentially about.

Finally, we turn to the first two chapters by **Moltmann** to anticipate briefly a few of the insights in store for the reader.

If there is any one note that comes through with unmistakable clarity it is Moltmann's conviction that the future of the church lies with the recovery of the ministry of the laity. The gifts of gracious service (charismata) are given to the entire Body, and discipleship is carried out as members become agents of Christ's ministry, answering the needs of the world with the gifts, talents, and training they have received. The biblical model of the servant people of God is undermined by clericalism, however. To be sure, "clericalism" in the form of clergy domination of political and economic life belongs to a bygone era, but it persists in other forms seemingly more benign but actually no less fateful. Wherever the church's ministry is understood as the responsibility primarily of professional leaders, clericalism is present. As such, this attitude is by no means confined to hierarchically organized churches. In spite of its avowal of the priesthood of all believers, the Reformation never succeeded in overcoming an essentially clerical understanding of the church. The preacher moved to center stage, and the life of the community continued to revolve around clerical leadership. Even congregationally governed churches do not seem immune but manifest the same tendency to think of the church as gathered about a strong personality who exercises clerical functions.

Obviously the clerical style of church leadership meets the needs of clergy and laity alike; it is more comfortable and congenial to human nature, else it would not be so persistent. Moltmann is convinced, however, that a reexamination of our practices, painful as this may be, is necessary in light of the gospel. With this in mind he turns to an analysis of the sacraments.

Rites and ceremonies reflect and embody definite understandings of the nature and purpose of the church. This fact causes Moltmann to raise some basic questions about present-day baptismal practices. Indeed baptism is a kind of test case for the method which Moltmann wants to apply to all areas of the church's life: *the dialectical relation of theory and practice.* As a *systematic* theologian he wants to know how theory (the Christian gospel) shapes and informs practice; as a *practical* theologian he wants to know how church life and practices influence the way people receive and understand the Christian gospel, the basic theory. Baptism provides a good case study to analyze both questions: What kind of church has shaped our current baptismal practices? And at the same time, what kind of church do our present practices tend to produce and perpetuate?

Moltmann is convinced that the practice of infant baptism reflects the Constantinian era of Christian history rather than the New Testament. It manifests a situation in which religious identity, like citizenship, was given by the state. Baptism into a state church is automatic. The result of this practice is "civil religion" and a church indistinguishable from the culture. Church membership is not a matter of decision nor does it demand sacrifice or service. Church membership tends to perpetuate, even in modern democracies, the fundamental medieval linkage between throne and altar. Religion serves to legitimate "the powers that be" in state and society and give the general populace a sense of moral order and continuity under a benevolent Providence.

If there is to be a change toward a creative and self-consciously innovative stance in the church, those rites and ceremonies that express in summary fashion the church's understanding of itself and its mission must also change. "Every change in theory demands a change in practice," says Moltmann. "Every change in practice requires a change in theory. Every change in theory and practice must bring a corresponding change in the rituals of life." If the church is to be an advance guard of the kingdom for which Jesus called, baptism will have to be a sign of enlistment rather than automatically being associated with birth, family, and tradition. It should be a matter of conscious commitment to a life of discipleship in a community under the lordship of Christ. This can be symbolized and expressed, claims Moltmann, only by a "baptism into Christian calling" *(Berufungstaufe)*, a baptism that celebrates the faith and discipline both of the community and of the one baptized.

It should be noted that Moltmann is not calling for "believers' baptism" in the usual sense. "It is not feelings of faith or experiences of conversion that are testified to through baptism," he says, "but the calling into which the person has entered," his or her vocation in the context of the kingdom. We cannot expect to produce a mature and responsible church as long as the ritual for entrance into the Body is primarily practiced with infants, he insists.

Regardless of whether one agrees with Moltmann's arguments, one cannot fail to be challenged by the way he puts his finger on a key methodological issue. Colloquially, we might represent his theory/praxis dialectic by saying, "What you practice is what you get." If we do not want a Constantinian church, perhaps we should look again at baptismal practices that took shape in the Constantinian era, testing them, not just by the needs of our own time, but by the New Testament with which they must accord.

Moltmann's suggestions regarding eucharistic practice are similarly arresting and thought-provoking. It is not the purpose of this introduction, however, to summarize the chapters that follow but merely to whet the appetite. Therefore I leave to the reader the satisfaction that comes from encountering new angles and points of view from which to reflect on age-old practices.

Let me conclude by calling attention to the clue given in the first chapter to the heart of Moltmann's thought. He chooses as his paradigm for ministry the care of the physically and mentally handicapped and the terminally ill. This seems an unlikely choice for the "theologian of hope." These are, after all, persons for whom there is little or no hope. Their future is already decided. Their possibilities are severely limited, if not nonexistent. Moreover, the one who ministers to them has little chance for the kind of recognition or positive feedback by which we usually measure our accomplishments in ministry. These persons cannot provide us with the success stories that we commonly use to demonstrate to ourselves and others the effectiveness of our counseling and care. However, asserts Moltmann, it is only as we learn to "die daily" to ego-satisfaction in terms of the values of this world (including the accolades of one's professional peer group), that we begin to participate in the depth of the sufferings of God in the world. This is a note which, though present in the *Theology of Hope,* did not come into its own until *The Crucified God,* yet undoubtedly it represents Moltmann's thought at its most sensitive. Like Bonhoeffer, Moltmann believes that "only the suffering God can help," and that "Christians range themselves with God in his suffering."[11]

This is not to say that suffering is of value in and of itself or that Christians are called to be masochists, for it is suffering—especially the suffering of the innocent—that is to be overcome in the kingdom of God. However, the way toward the kingdom leads inevitably through the cross. Christians voluntarily assume some of the burden of those who suffer by identifying with them. In an existence that continues to be imperfect, they protest against suffering as a cruel and meaningless fate by turning it into a shared burden that can be confronted and partially overcome by the human spirit indwelt by the divine Spirit of caring love. Thus our small victories participate in and are promissory signs of that day when "God shall wipe away every tear." The sovereignty of death is broken by the power of love that is willing to coparticipate in death by virtue of the strength promised in the resurrection.

To read Moltmann, both in these chapters and in the much larger corpus of his works now available in English, is to be challenged on every level, not only in theory but in practice, not only in our intellectual reflections but in our daily rounds, not only in our work but in our prayers. And that is good theology—good practical theology!

The Diaconal Church in the Context of the Kingdom of God
Jürgen Moltmann

My thesis is a simple one: *The local congregation is the future of the church.* The renewal of the church finally depends upon what happens at the grass-roots level. And renewal at this level awaits, it seems to me, the conscious reclaiming of the gifts of the Spirit on the part of the laity. These gifts, which in the New Testament are always identified as signs of the coming kingdom of God, are given to the whole people of God for ministry, for *diakonia.*

The New Testament concept of diakonia is too important to be limited to those in the ordained ministry. A "deacon" is one who serves. But the whole church—not just its ordained members—is called to service, to a diaconate in the world. In understanding the church as "the servant people of God" it is especially important to remember that the in-breaking of God's kingdom is the context within which service takes place. A diaconate in the context of the Kingdom is service in discipleship to the crucified Christ—and in no other name! While service in discipleship to the Crucified One is diakonia in the context of the coming of God's kingdom—and in no other context!

When we speak of the kingdom of God we must avoid two errors. We are not looking at our own works and their success. The results of merely human efforts would be a human kingdom—but no kingdom of *God.* Even the church constitutes no kingdom of glory in this world. However, when we speak of the kingdom of God and of God's lordship, neither are we looking in faith to an invisible world in the beyond, a consolation that enables us in this lonely veil of tears to carry our cross and fulfill our duty.

If we want to speak in a Christian manner of the kingdom of God and his lordship, then we must look to Jesus alone and not to ourselves, to his history and not to our own. Only in community with Jesus does the lordship of God become a liberating power and his Kingdom become the goal that fulfills all our hopes. In the fellowship of Jesus, the kingdom of God becomes more than simply an inspiration in the midst of the battles of this world and also something different than just a yearning for another world.

The Reality of the Kingdom

How are we to recognize the kingdom of God in Jesus, and where are we to find it in fellowship with him?

We recognize the kingdom first of all in the mission of Jesus. The Synoptic Gospels present the life story of Jesus in the light of his messianic mission, and they present his messianic mission in the light of his proclamation of the gospel. According to Isaiah 35 and Isaiah 61, the Messiah's mission includes the healing of those who are sick and abandoned: "The blind receive their sight and the lame walk, lepers are cleansed and the deaf hear, and the dead are raised up, and the poor have good news preached to them" (Matt. 11:5, *cf.* 10:8 and Luke 4:18). Whenever and wherever this happens we can know that his Kingdom is coming.

All of Jesus' efforts and activities are directed toward his mission: proclamation, healing, summoning and collecting together a group of followers—all of these took place, according to the understanding of his disciples, within an all-encompassing meaning or mission. As a result, everything done in his name is mission, and all Christian mission is a participation in *his* mission to the world. Any division between proclamation (kerygma) and service (diakonia) would split the unity out of which Jesus worked and to which he called his disciples. Healing the sick and driving out demons, setting at liberty those in prison and giving sight to the blind, the hunger for righteousness and the liberation of the oppressed—all of these belong to Jesus' own mission and therefore are also aspects of the mission of his disciples. These actions go with the proclamation of the good news to the poor, and in that context they gain their messianic quality.

What is this gospel that Jesus proclaims and enacts? If we are to understand Jesus' proclamation of the Kingdom against its Old Testament background (Isa. 52), his gospel both announces and sets into motion the messianic age. It "says to Zion, 'Your God reigns' " (Isa. 52:7). God exercises his lordship over his people, and, because this people are lost and imprisoned in exile, his seizure of power is a freeing and saving act. His act frees them from servitude to oppressive powers and delivers them from an eclipse of the divine. The gospel is nothing less than the call to freedom: "Shake yourself from the dust, arise, O captive Jerusalem; loose the bonds from your neck, O captive daughter of Zion" (Isa. 52:2). When God comes, the impossible becomes possible: bonds bind no more, one can break free from them; weaknesses enervate no more, one can take possession of one's strengths; dust no longer holds one down, one can shake free from it. Where God is king, human beings are released for their own freedom. The gospel is therefore at one and the same time the proclamation of God's sovereignty and the call to human freedom. "The time is fulfilled, and the kingdom of God is at hand; repent, and believe in the gospel" (Mark 1:15).

Because the gospel announces the coming God and the liberation of humanity, the new eschatological exodus into the promised land and the founding of a new creation begins with this proclamation (*cf.* Isa. 52–66). It calls for the exodus of humanity out of its slavery, a slavery for which humanity itself has been responsible, into the freedom of the Kingdom. And just as the first exodus of Israel out of Egypt was accompanied by "signs and wonders," so also this second, eschatological exodus will be accompanied by signs and wonders. Those who take part in it can tell of the signs and wonders which they have experienced in the history of Jesus, in the history of the apostles, and in their own life history right down to the present.

We recognize the kingdom of God in Jesus, therefore, when we recognize his mission and let it have its effect on us. We recognize his mission when we hear the call of freedom, and it initiates that work with which the future of God begins in us.

But *where* do we find the kingdom of God according to Jesus?

The Location of the Kingdom

Jesus' gospel points us clearly to "the poor." His Beatitudes identify them as those to whom the Kingdom belongs. Jesus, the one who heals the sick, who takes the lepers to himself, who is the "friend of sinners and outcasts," shows all too clearly where the kingdom of God is to be discovered—not at the top where the leading members of the society are to be found, where the rich, the healthy, and the talented congratulate themselves—but at the bottom, in the darkness, where no one notices. As Christoph Blumhardt once commented, Jesus grasps human society, so to say, "from its underside." Blumhardt was convinced that the quality of a society is best revealed in the quality of its hospitals, its mental institutions, its prisons.

Sickness is a sign of the fragile constitution of humanity. From the beginning of Jesus' activity until the end, people with all imaginable manner of illness came to Jesus—from fever to blindness, from lameness to leprosy. In the company of Jesus we discover indeed the whole misery of humankind. The possessed, the crippled, the lame, the blind, the hungry, the guilty—all emerge from the dark corners of society into which they have been banned, or in which they have concealed themselves out of their own anxiety. They appear because they have been attracted by the life which Jesus extends to those around him through his love. They recognize him as the Messiah because he becomes their hope. It is not that they come to the kingdom of God; rather, the Kingdom comes to them in the form of the Son of man who accepts them and takes them to himself. What does all of this mean?

1. On earth the kingdom of God begins with the poor, the

sick, and the lepers, the outcasts who are excluded from normal society. The New Testament speaks in terms of conflict in the world—the conflict between the healthy and sick, the righteous and sinners, the rich and poor, Pharisees and publicans—and strangely enough always in a *one-sided* way! Those who are well do not need a physician but rather the sick; there is more joy over one sinner who repents than over ninety-nine righteous; poor Lazarus goes to Abraham's bosom while the rich man goes to hell; the publican goes home justified, the Pharisee does not. "Why this one-sidedness?" one might ask. In a one-sided, inhuman world of conflict, the saving element can only be represented by a reality which is also one-sided that brings about God's righteousness by redressing the balance.

2. If the poor, the sick, and the rejected are called "blessed," then they are not the *objects* of Christian charity, generosity, and love. They are rather first of all fellow members of the Kingdom (Matt. 5:3) and "brothers" of the Son of man, who will judge the world (Matt. 25:31 ff.). They must be respected for their dignity, honor, and worth; therefore they are *subjects* in the kingdom of God, not the objects of our sympathy. Every act of help is preceded by our fellowship in common, and every act of caring has its origins in Christian friendship. Before you can be for others you must live with others.

We find the kingdom of God with Jesus when we enter into community with the poor, the sick, the sorrowing, and the guilty, recognizing them as fellow members of the Kingdom, and are accepted by them as their brothers and sisters. But to find the Kingdom in this way inevitably means at the same time a critique of the rich and the healthy, the self-satisfied and self-righteous. And this critique always means some alienation from the present order of things. Indeed, "alienation" may well be the form which biblical "self-denial" takes in our day.

The Healing and Saving Power of the Kingdom

What is the kingdom of God as we find it specifically in Jesus' relation to the sick? As the ancient word "Savior" implies, Jesus brings the kingdom of God to the poor, the sick, and the guilty, as their healing. According to the prophets, whoever announces with authority the messianic time of salvation also heals wounds. The words *yasha* and *yeshuah* in the Old Testament, and the words *sozo* and *soteria* in the New Testament, mean to save, to heal, and to free. Salvation is actually healing, and healing is the concrete result of saving. Therefore an event (saving) and its results (salvation), an action (healing), and its effects (health), belong inseparably together. The Savior brings salvation precisely through his healing action that takes disturbed and fragmented lives and makes them whole again. In his messianic mission, announcing the good news (i.e., evangelizing) and doing the good news (i.e., diakonia) belong together as the one comprehensive work of the God who comes near to us in Christ in order to deal with the entirety of human suffering and death. For this reason one ought not to make the old metaphysical distinction between time and eternity, salvation and human welfare, word and deed, church and state, faith and reason, in such a way as to spiritualize salvation in a platonic manner by reducing it to the salvation of the soul alone. "Today salvation has come to this house!" (Luke 19:9). Whoever seeks to divide this reality divides what God has joined together and made whole. There are no needs which are simply external or purely physical. "The body is meant . . . for the Lord, and the Lord for the body" (I Cor. 6:13). Salvation means to become whole; it means to unite that which was divided and split, disturbed and distorted, and make it "right" again. This is as true of a distorted relationship to oneself and to others as it is of a disturbed relationship to God. With regard to salvation, therefore, one can only think holistically. And the nature of Christian salvation demands that we also live and act in a holistic way. The kind of thinking that makes distinctions between salvation and human welfare, between inner life and external reality, between soul and body, does not reflect the holistic nature of salvation, but reflects instead the sickness of division. If we do not overcome in our thinking the kind of mentality which divides and isolates and abstracts, how can we expect to overcome the misery caused in our lives by these divisions?

Diakonia in the context of the kingdom of God is therefore service of a comprehensive and holistic nature. This is the only way it can correspond to the unity of the Kingdom and the oneness of the Creator. Holistic diakonia is healing action directed toward all of the unhealthy distortions and estrangements of human existence, whether in personal, social, or religious life. Diakonia in the context of the Kingdom is a realistic ministry of reconciliation (II Cor. 5:18). What is separated is brought together again, and peace is found in the midst of strife.

Diakonia under the Cross

Now let us apply what we have said thus far to a test case: our ministry to those in so-called hopeless situations, the incurably ill. We get some clue as to what is involved in such a ministry in the declaration of purpose formulated by the founders of the Brotherhood of Nazareth, which operates institutions for epileptics and the mentally ill in Bethel, Germany. According to their declaration of purpose, entrance into the task of diakonia to the handicapped demands readiness to suffer and die. "Love toward God and toward the Savior strengthens us to do what the natural man is not able to do—to die daily." The care of epileptics and the mentally ill "places before each the choice of simply abandoning this kind of ministry or learning daily how to die." This "dying daily" certainly does not refer to any kind of arbitrary exercise of piety. Nor is it, I believe, only a poetic expression borrowed from the mysticism of the cross. Instead it speaks of a real experience: the experience that incurable illness is an anticipation of death which is transmitted to the one who is with the incurable person. Friedrich von Bodelschwingh, Sr., the founder of Bethel, understood the ministry to epilepsy patients as a battle with death. What shall one hope when there is nothing more to hope for? How can one help where there is nothing help can do? In such encounters one cannot transmit health to the sick or hope to those who are in despair. In such a situation one cannot be sustained by the prospect of success in life. The sickness is shared even with the healthy, despair stalks the one who hopes, and death reaches out toward the living. It is then that we begin to learn, if we persist and do not flee, what it means to "die daily." Gradually that self in us dies which would like to be reinforced through work and occasionally a little success and appreciation. Gradually the ego, built up by doing and having, dies. And, as the cemetery at Bethel shows, in the end those who are the helpers themselves die—many of them when they were still very young—and there in the cemetery is portrayed that final covenant and fellowship between the deacons and the sick whom they serve.

Now we can of course ask, Are the incurably sick really helped when those who would serve become sick through them? Moreover, where can we receive the resources for this willingness to die, for this willingness to give up one's own self, one's ego, and quite possibly one's own life?

The Secret of Healing

The secret of the kind of healing that leads to holistic salvation is to be found in the saying: "Wounds are healed through wounds." Not through his superiority to sickness, suffering, and death does Jesus help us, but through his giving himself over to suffering and his obedience unto death on the cross. The idols of power and success are of no more help in the hospital. Fundamentally only the suffering God can help, for only he loves in a fully selfless way. "Surely he has borne our sicknesses and carried our sorrows," reads the alternative translation of Isaiah 53:4. "And with his wounds we are healed" (v. 5). In the story of the suffering of Jesus we recognize the suffering of divine love. Out of his suffering we receive life; out of his death, healing. Precisely in this way God is actively and intensely creative as he takes upon himself in the strength of his love the suffering, rejection, and death of his creation. It is when Jesus falls silent on the cross that he speaks to us with the greatest intensity.

Ordinarily we divide suffering into that which can be

eliminated and that which cannot, just as we divide illnesses into those that can be cured and those that cannot. There is another dimension of suffering, which we usually conceal from ourselves, but in which we are nonetheless constantly involved. It is the suffering we shift to others. For example, we overcome our own hunger—and let others hunger for us. We immunize ourselves against natural diseases—and become ever more subject to the diseases of civilization. In this way we constantly transfer the burden of suffering to other persons or to other areas of the body while giving the impression that we are overcoming suffering.

The messianic secret concerning healing is just the opposite of the pattern which copes with suffering by relegating it to others. It is suffering freely taken upon oneself in order that others might live. This free assuming of suffering and failure, and the free acceptance of suffering in behalf of others is the transfiguration of suffering. It is no longer destructive; rather it unites. It does not isolate anymore; it binds together. The suffering and death of Jesus on the cross have always been experienced by faith as uniquely healing suffering.

The suffering of the Son of God is reconciling suffering; his death is an atoning, justifying sacrifice. Therefore, those who follow Jesus in his messianic mission are not required to take *his* cross and *his* death upon themselves. For the reconciling of the world God alone has done enough. However, Christians are called to take up their cross. "If any man would come after me, let him deny himself and take up his cross and follow me" (Mark 8:34). What is meant is that each of us has waiting for us in our lives a measure of suffering which we are called upon to assume in solidarity with all who suffer. Whoever no longer seeks to shift suffering to others, whoever takes on suffering, whoever suffers with others, whoever removes suffering from others, such a person heals and spreads peace to others around him or her. Such a person is in the deepest sense "healthy," even if he or she dies as a result. From this person others also gain health. But where are we to receive strength for such voluntary identification with weakness and sickness?

The Power That Heals

I want to speak now of a source without which such dying daily cannot be taken on oneself: *prayer and meditation*. If we throw ourselves into ministry or social work because we cannot come to terms with ourselves, in the end we will only become a burden to ourselves and others. Persons who want to help and to do things for others or for the world without deepening their own self-understanding, freedom, and ability to love, will find they have nothing to give to others. Even with good intentions they will communicate only their own yearning for identity, their anxiety, aggression and ambitions, their ideological prejudices, etc. The person who wants to fill an inner emptiness through service to others will only spread this emptiness further. Why? Because every one of us has an effect on others much less through what we do than through who we are—although in our activism we often fail to recognize this fact. Only those who have found themselves can give themselves. Only those who have grasped the meaning of life can act meaningfully. Only those who have become free within from self-seeking, from preoccupation with self, and from anxiety about life, can share suffering and take it upon themselves—and free others.

Communion with Jesus leads us into service and into prayer, and love and prayer mutually reinforce and deepen each other. How does this occur? The more one loves the earth, the more one is sensitive to the misery of the sick, the abandoned, and the disturbed—as *one's own* misery! For *love finds the suffering of others insufferable*. One can no longer see it without being affected by it. One cannot simply become accustomed to it and overlook it.

If love makes us sensitive to the suffering of others then it leads us also into continuous prayer. We mourn with those who mourn and cry out with the wounded. How is prayer better described than as the grieving of the abandoned, the agony of those who are hurt, and the silence of the despairing—all of which cry out to God?

Likewise, the more spontaneously and passionately one prays and cries out to God, the deeper he will be drawn into the suffering of others. Praying in the Spirit, and intense love and concern for the life of the sick reinforce each other mutually and deepen the experience of the Spirit. Prayer does not compensate when love is lacking, nor can feverish involvement exempt us from praying.

Communion with Jesus leads at one and the same time, therefore, into action and into contemplation. We experience his presence in the tension between the silence of contemplation and the intensity of active battle. We become immersed in the contemplation of the Crucified One and forget ourselves—until we find ourselves once again in him. We become aware of the presence of the resurrected Christ in the depth of our soul and experience his spiritual presence. Our consciousness becomes broadened to include that dimension which in the hustle and bustle of active life remains underdeveloped. Meditation and contemplation destroy the fetish we have made out of our success-oriented activities. They destroy the idolatry we have made out of the pursuit of happiness. They make our service to others more humane because they make us more humane. We can understand our own identity as a freed and redeemed identity received from God, and with quiet certainty we can take our place and assume our responsibilities within the redeeming history of God with the world. We are then able to see everything—the living and the dead, the healthy and the sick—as transfigured in the light of the resurrection world of God. I am not referring to peculiar mystical illuminations or mystical experiences of love but rather to the fact that diakonia—precisely as it is directed toward the incurably ill and is for that reason associated with our own "dying daily"—is transformed because it is done in the name of, and with the help of, the One who is "the resurrection and the life."

Diakonia as servanthood under the cross means, therefore, to participate in suffering, to accept suffering, and to take on the suffering of others. Such service involves the daily death of the ego and its anxieties. Service under the cross happens in the presence and power of the Resurrected One. For it is only the resurrection hope that makes us ready for selfless love and dying.

Diakonia in the Power of the Holy Spirit

Diakonia is rooted in the community of Christ. For Paul the congregation is the place of the revelation of the Spirit in all the colorful variety of different spiritual gifts, or *charismata*. For him the Christian community itself is defined as a fellowship movement of that Spirit which will be poured out on all flesh. Not only prophets, priests, and kings, but in the messianic age the whole people of God—men and women, Jews and Gentiles, slaves and masters, the sick and the healthy—will be filled with the life-giving, creative power of God. In the events of Pentecost the promises of the prophet Joel begin to be fulfilled.

Notice that in describing these powers and gifts of the new creation in I Corinthians 12, Paul avoids the terms "office," "vocation," or "function" and chooses the expression diakonia instead. "There are varieties of services" (v. 5). This corresponds to his portrayal of Jesus in the second chapter of Philippians. The one who is exalted Lord above all is at the same time the humble servant of all. Matthew 20:25-28 states it succinctly: "You know that the rulers of the Gentiles lord it over them, and their great men exercise authority over them. It shall not be so among you; but whoever would be great among you must be your servant, and whoever would be first among you must be your slave; even as the Son of man came not to be served but to serve, and to give his life as ransom for many."

Before the Christian community begins to practice diaconal service toward others, however, it must of necessity be within itself a caring community. "It is toward its own members already a diaconal community or it is no community."[1] The charismatic community is by definition a serving community, and vice versa. The ordinary laws of social stratification and the struggle for recognition and power cease when members begin to serve one another with their best efforts and together live out of the servanthood of Jesus. This is why the Christian community emerges as a new creation, marked by reconciliation, in places where previously alienation, oppression, and death reigned. The new reality is a community created out of women and men, Greeks and barbarians, slaves and masters, the strong and the weak, the healthy and the sick—even the fellowship of the living and the dead (Gal. 3:28, Rom. 10:12, I Cor. 1:26, Rom. 14:9). The diaconal community is not a club or association formed to care for its own kind. In Christ, all the walls that encourage us to consider ourselves better than others are broken down.

The Pitfalls of Specialization

The specialized ministry of the care of the sick has its roots in the diaconal nature of the Christian community itself. Any special ministries are grounded in the common ministry of all of the faithful, just as the special office of the priest is grounded in the universal priesthood of all believers.

If we agree with this theologically, some practical implications follow: Diakonia and healing occur through community and in the community. Specialized diaconal institutions are justified, therefore, only if they do not usurp the responsibility of every local congregation to be a center of caring service.

We have not taken seriously enough the healing power of the community. Technological-scientific medicine heals by isolating—in an isolation ward or intensive care unit. Just as important as technical care, however, is human contact which combats anxiety and loneliness. Our encounters with African and Asian medicine through the ecumenical movement have opened our eyes to the importance of this holistic approach.

Work with the handicapped has clearly shown for example that in the suffering of such persons a distinction can be made between the physical handicaps themselves and the social consequences. Anxiety, aggression, being looked down upon, isolation—the social consequences—are often the worse hindrance. To be sure, without the physical handicap these would not be. But it should be possible to have the physical limitations without the adverse social effects. The social obstacles can be overcome only through the recognition and acceptance of the handicapped in human fellowship. More and more it is recognized that specialized handling and expert treatment are not sufficient because they do not eliminate social isolation. Instead they often only reinforce and deepen it. Living and working communities that bring the handicapped together with those who are not are very important, therefore, to effect social rehabilitation.

There has been a tendency in the history of the church to professionalize services. Pastors and missionaries are set apart, specialists are trained to serve as social workers, and hospitals, orphanages, and homes for the aged are developed. The end result of this greater specialization is to turn diakonia into something done by professionals rather than by the whole congregation. The congregation participates through its giving, to be sure, but the members are for the most part at least one step removed from the immediate experience of ministry and service. Professionally trained people become an ersatz for the laity as a whole and enable the average member to assume that he has taken care of his responsibility to serve simply by paying his money. Yet this practice of delegating our service to others makes the local Christian congregation poor and even sick.

The wider implications of what we are saying apply also to the staffing of the local church, where a similar phenomenon can be observed. The more professional persons are hired, the more the tendency is for the laity to leave to them the responsibility for the life of the church, and as a result lay members become ever more passive. One realizes too late that through this process the charismatic fullness and variety of the Christian fellowship are lost to our experience. After all, it was not just Marx, but Schiller and Hölderlin as well, who in the last century saw specialization as a chief cause of alienation. Although specialized professional training is necessary today, it must not be allowed to become an end in itself. The specialist must as soon as possible become integrated not only within his own person but in the wholeness and interdependence of the body which is the church. Where specialization is sought as the answer, the congregation becomes a passive object of service rather than being the active subject. We need to ask ourselves whether adding professional persons to church staffs is a step toward the Kingdom or a step backward.

All of our attempts at achieving fellowship in the church will be for naught if we do not recognize that diakonia and fellowship are basically inseparable. Fellowship and community come into being when persons live with one another and in the power of the Spirit are for one another. Here lies the root of all Christian diakonia, the sharing of the gifts and graces which make actual the universal priesthood of all believers. Diakonia is the life-form of the community of Christ, and in such a community Christ himself becomes an actuality through diaconal life.

Those who are in the professional ministry must resist the tendency found in all of our churches to professionalize diakonia to an ever-greater extent and insist that the service of the people of God be shared by all. It is indeed the responsibility of the professional ministry to find ways and means by which the ministry of the whole community can become effective and meaningful so that each one has his or her share in the enterprise.

Society in the Context of the Kingdom of God

I would be remiss if I did not conclude by applying the perspective that I have developed with regard to the congregation to the larger society where we can see some of the same forces and problems at work.

In society as a whole we see a similar tendency to turn over to functionaries and bureaucratic apparatuses the responsibilities which we all ought to carry as citizens. As a result our western societies suffer from the same increasing passivity in the citizenry that we have observed as a phenomenon in the church. As more and more responsibility for our lives is taken over by bureaucracies, human beings have less and less a sense of determining their own destinies. Persons must become the subjects of their own histories again; they must see themselves and their actions as having an important role in shaping their future in order to realize their worth as human beings. The burden of responsibility cannot be taken from us and delegated to others without finally dehumanizing us.

Therefore the church ought to applaud and encourage all efforts at local initiative which seek to solve problems and carry out services on the local level without recourse to huge bureaucracies for solving all problems. This is not to say that bureaucracies are unnecessary. One way the larger, more impersonal structures of our society can be kept human, however, is through education in the personalization of ministry and service that the church can encourage by training its members in diakonia on the local level.

In this respect the Christian community becomes "a seed sown in hope" in the larger society, for we believe that the kind of hope and anticipation of new life that is possible in service under the cross and in the power of the Spirit will be infectious, and will finally bring to this apathetic, discouraged, and frustrated society, a new hope in the power of life against death.

I have sought to describe the resources for the diaconal church that are to be found in the fundamental Christian gospel which begins with an announcement of the coming of the kingdom of God. That Kingdom is breaking in where we least expect it, among the poor and oppressed, the sick and the lonely, those who in the eyes of this world are of little or no account. But the power of the Kingdom is to be found precisely where we participate as a church in the pattern of the cross of Christ, in which God gives up his honor and glory and comes into the midst of our suffering world to identify with those who are in need. The service to the sick, especially to those suffering from incurable disease, is a kind of paradigm of the radical nature of Christian diakonia. For here we see how it is necessary for us to die daily, not hoping for the usual signs of success and worldly acclaim for our efforts, but out of love and the power of the Spirit to be willing to minister in what the world calls "hopeless situations."

Thus the Christian community in her diaconal ministry is precisely that sign of hope in a hopeless world which we profoundly believe God will use to accomplish his saving work among us today.

The Life Signs of the Spirit in the Fellowship Community of Christ
Jürgen Moltmann

The *future of the church* is a topic that concerns all of us. Yet it is a subject upon which we cannot reflect without some prior analysis of the present condition of the church and the developments from the past that have brought the church to her present state. Otherwise all our projected hopes for the future of the church would remain in the realm of dreams and speculations removed from reality.

If I speak primarily out of the European situation, it is because that is the part of the church I know best. My purpose, however, is to stimulate my readers to reflect on the future of the church in their own situations and to combine their hope for the church with their own concrete experience of the church.

If, as we saw in the previous chapter, the future of the church lies with the recovery of the ministries of the local congregation, the renewal of the worship life that grounds and undergirds those ministries becomes all-important. Part of my purpose in this chapter, therefore, is to understand Word and sacrament anew in the context of the congregation and from that context to interpret them afresh.

From Christian Fellowship to Established Church

In Europe and the sections of Latin America previously under European colonialism, we encounter Christianity in the form of established, largely nationalized, churches. In

37

the New Testament, however, we find Christianity in the shape of voluntary fellowships in the midst of various nations, races, and cultures. This is an important difference. Since our ability to understand texts out of the past is limited by our present situation, it would seem that contemporary churches are closed to a full understanding of the documents of the New Testament. At the same time, to the degree that those same texts provide critical distance from our present situation, we will tend to be alienated from our own established churches. The conflict between contemporary ecclesiastical Christianity and its own biblical sources can be resolved only if we are willing to exercise criticism of certain historical decisions and where necessary free ourselves from them.

The first historical shape of Christianity was the Jewish-Christian congregation that gathered around "the twelve apostles" and understood itself as a messianic renewal movement within the twelve tribes of Israel. The *first historical decision* of Christianity was the decision to become a mission to the Gentiles and a "fellowship of Jews and Gentiles," as evident in the case of Stephen and "the Seven" and in the form Christianity took at Antioch. Both the conflict between Peter and Paul, and the council of the apostles in Jerusalem, reflect the importance of this decision. The term *ekklēsia* was used for the first time in Antioch to describe the "congregation of Jews and Gentiles"—i.e., Gentiles did not have to become Jews in order to be Christians, nor did Jews have to become Gentiles. Used originally to refer to the political assembly of the citizens of a city, the term *ekklēsia* now designated a unique new reality. Christianity was neither a Jewish sect nor a hellenistic cultic community but a *tertium quid*. It was organized as a voluntary fellowship without regard to the distinctions of religion, race, class, nation, or gender, that divided the ancient world. "There is neither Jew nor Greek, there is neither slave nor free, there is neither male nor female; for you are all one in Christ Jesus" (Gal. 3:28). Because of this the church spread quickly and irresistibly; she was the concrete form of freedom and peace. The second historical form Christianity took, therefore, was that of a community open to the world, one that offered an independent communal existence in contrast to the traditional lines of division and enmity.

The *second historic decision,* however, was the transition of Christianity into the Roman imperial church with the advent of the so-called "Constantinian era." This change has determined the shape of the church in most Christian countries down to the present day. The fellowship of Christ became the religion of society. The church forfeited her special form and distinct visibility as a fellowship and became a part of the public order. She was no longer composed of voluntary, independent congregations but was defined by belonging to regions, provinces, and parochial divisions of cities. Because parochial districts are not fellowships, the offices of priest and bishop took on the character of civil authorities. The division between clergy and laity was finalized. Faith was exercised through participation in the religious ceremonies sponsored by the church. Fellowship *in* the church was replaced by gradations of communion *with* the church. The hierarchy became the essence of the church, and the people of God became "the faithful," i.e., lay supporters of the clergy. The gospel witness became an official proclamation handed down from higher authorities. With this came also the deterioration of Christian diakonia practiced by the congregation. It was replaced by public welfare and private charity. The Christian mission of evangelization was also lost. It was supplanted by forced Christianization of conquered peoples in the name of the political religion of Christendom—"for the Blessed Virgin and the King of Spain!" The sacramental life signs of the Holy Spirit in the koinonia (communion) with Christ were turned into the sacraments of the church and understood to be official prerogatives and duties of the spiritual leaders; the clergy would dispense spiritual gifts to the common folk who by implication lacked the Spirit. In the place of the community of Christ in the midst of the people was the institutional church and its religious care of the people.

The contradiction within the church can be described in this way: As Constantine turned a persecuted faith into a "permitted religion" and his successors made it the "official religion," the whole Roman empire was opened up to the mission and expansion of Christianity. Yet for this the church paid a high price: she had to take on the role of being a unifying state religion for the Roman empire. In this way the church "reached" all humanity. But as what—the fellowship of Jesus or the religious system that complemented the prevailing social system?

The Rediscovery of the Congregation

Undoubtedly, religious power is experienced in the church understood as a hierarchy or as under clerical management, but the image engendered is that of an all-wise, all-powerful, divine Lord in heaven. God as love, however, can only be witnessed to and experienced in a congregation small enough for members to know each other and accept one another as they are accepted by Christ. The gospel of Christ crucified for us puts an end to religion as power and opens up the possibility of experiencing God in the context of genuine community as the God of love. Justification by faith puts an end to religious bondage and creates freedom in fellowship. Therefore, instead of involuntary membership in the church, as characterizes most of the established churches of Europe, membership should result from freely chosen identification with a fellowship. It is possible even within large, impersonal parishes to build identifiable, smaller fellowship groups. Justification by faith should also mean that church leaders share decision-making with the congregation and practice collegial and collective leadership in the Spirit. Sharing and mutual sympathy would not be limited to the Sunday morning service, but would permeate everyday life as well.

The full integration of the clergy into the congregation has another implication. The pastor is first and foremost a member of the fellowship and only subsequently, and on this basis, is he or she called to a certain office. Specialized tasks in the congregation presuppose the common calling of each and every member, for the community of Christ is a charismatic community. Its genuinely communal nature can only be seen, however, to the extent that the hierarchy and leadership—including theologians—are really integrated into the local congregation. The larger church organization must be understood in this same way. Nothing should be unrelated to the local fellowship. Service, mission, ecumenical outreach—all of these belong in the congregation, and responsibility for them should not be shifted to agencies beyond the local chuch in such a way as to relieve ordinary Christians of their involvement. Likewise, the task of theological reflection should not be the restricted province of university and seminary faculties, but should be done in the congregation. We have delegated too many tasks to specialists. As a result, our own strengths atrophy. Initially it seems like a relief when a congregation employs an additional trained clergyperson to take over a ministry. But the end result is too often alienation from our own possibilities. Only to the degree that the congregation becomes the conscious agent of its history with God in the Holy Spirit will it become mature and responsible. Then we no longer have "Reverend Jones' church," but a congregation that is awake to its own history and hope and lives out its own history.

Such a development can have socio-political implications. The charismatic congregation that becomes conscious of its own powers and tasks overcomes the clergy-laity gap. It overcomes within its own life the kind of alienation that is produced by the division of labor. In a society in which class divisions and privileges continue to be promoted by the intensification of the division of labor and specialization, the church can present the hope for a more human future only as it is such a charismatic congregation.

The congregation in which the people are conscious agents of their history with God overcomes the religious passivity which results from political oppression. In such a congregation basic democracy is practiced. The free church congregations that arose out of the English Revolution were the ferment of political democracy—and still are today. Such congregations can become the source of the fundamental democratic renewal of society if they continue to spawn grass-roots efforts to liberate the poor, heal the sick, and free the oppressed. Both in "representative" democracies bogged down with bureaucratization and in socialist lands burdened with paternalistic party leadership, the church as a communal fellowship can represent the hope for a future that is more free.

The Sacraments and the Sacrament

If the future of the church and its contribution to the world lies in the recovery of genuine fellowship within the congregation, the traditional rites and ceremonies of the congregation must be rethought from this perspective in the light of the proclamation of the gospel.

The hermeneutical method I follow moves from biblical exegesis through systematic reflection to suggestions for the practical life of the church. Interpretation of the biblical origins of the Christian faith must be done with one eye toward the actual historical results of Christianity. And these results in turn must be tested for their consistency with biblical sources. There is no interpretation of Scripture which is not at the same time an interpretation of our own situation, and no Christian interpretation of our situation without dialogue with the Scriptures. This is the so-called "hermeneutical circle"—except for the fact that it loses its circular character when our understanding of the Bible and of ourselves is informed by a knowledge of the Kingdom which the scriptures promise and for which faith hopes. Let us apply this method now to the life of the congregation as we focus on the sacraments.

The sacramental means of grace have traditionally been understood as those "sacramental acts" which were instituted by Christ and are intended to mediate salvation to human beings. The divine words of institution and promise take the elements and turn them into sacrament.

The Eastern church has never laid down the number of sacraments in any definitive way, though everything in the life of those churches is related to the liturgy and the eucharist. The Roman Catholic church identifies seven sacraments—"no more and no less"—according to the Council of Trent. The churches of the Reformation identify as means of salvation: Word, Baptism, and the Lord's

Supper. However only Baptism and the Lord's Supper qualify as sacraments.

Today the attempt is being made to understand sacraments theologically in light of their common origin. Karl Rahner calls the church itself the "fundamental sacrament" *(Grundsakrament)* and Christ the "original sacrament" *(Ursakrament)*. In a similar way Karl Barth calls the Incarnation the "one great Christian mystery and sacrament." The humanity of Christ is "the first sacrament." In his later works Barth eliminates the use of the concept of sacrament and speaks only of "witnesses" *(Bezeugungen)*, because the reconciliation between God and humanity that occurred in Christ is the "unique, single sacrament accomplished once for all."[1] While in the past the doctrine of sacraments was characterized by positivistic and legalistic thinking and understanding, today we can observe on the basis of a christological understanding of the sacraments certain convergences in the Protestant and Catholic positions. We want to examine whether this convergence can help us further in our understanding of the genuine nature of the sacraments and sacramental practice in the Christian community.

Mystery and Its Revelation

The expression "sacrament" does not occur in the New Testament. In fact there is no comprehensive concept of sacramental acts. When the Greek word *mysterion* is translated by the Latin *sacramentum*, neither baptism nor the Lord's Supper is what is meant, but rather the eschatological secret of God.[2] *Mysterion* is an apocalyptic concept that refers to the future of the world hidden in the counsels of God. In terms of divine decisions this future was the first event in history; in terms of the unfolding of history it is the last event. The New Testament regards Jesus, his mission, his passion, and his resurrection from the dead, as *the* apocalypse (unveiling) of the divine mystery. Through him is given in the midst of history the decisive clue to the end of history. How is this future of God already revealed through Christ? By the gift of the Holy Spirit which is a mark of the end time. Where and how is this power of the new creation experienced? Through the Word, the community, and the "signs and wonders" of the messianic age. If Jesus himself is "the secret of divine sovereignty," then the signs of the messianic age belong to his own mystery. As Bornkamm has shown, the expression *mysterion* is used christologically, but with an unusual eschatological dimension. It reaches beyond Christ into the history of the Spirit and eschatological history. If, as we believe, this use of language in the New Testament is not accidental but is grounded in the nature of the reality expressed, the result is a somewhat different picture of the foundation for sacraments than the usual basis in ecclesiology and christology. What we call sacraments are in truth the "signs and wonders of the messianic age" that began with the sending of Jesus, continued in the experience of the Spirit, and will be completed in the kingdom of God. "Signs and wonders" accompanied Israel's exodus out of Egypt. Signs and wonders, say the prophets, will accompany the new exodus of Israel. As the book of Acts shows, the early Christian congregations understood their history in communion with Jesus as an eschatological exodus out of a world system that is passing away into the new creation of God. Their sacraments were "signs of the times": concentrated exodus experiences, treasured memories of Christ, and acts of hope directed toward the coming Kingdom. Therefore we can best call these early Christian sacraments, "signs of life in the Holy Spirit."

The Gospel and the Messianic Age

The word, *euangelion,* as used and understood in the New Testament, reflects Deutero-Isaiah and the apocalyptic literature which that writer influenced. According to that view, the messianic messenger precedes the coming of God's sovereignty and announces this coming as the "good news." In the Messiah's proclamation the lordship of God takes effect through the medium of the Word and awakens the freedom of faith, the passion of love, and the patience of hope. According to Isaiah 52, evangelizing has three dimensions. First, the assertion of *God's sovereignty* over his people and their history: "Say to Zion, 'Your God reigns' " (52:7). Second, the call *out of slavery into freedom:* "Loose the bonds from your neck, O captive daughter of Zion" (52:2). Third, both dimensions together—divine sovereignty and human liberation—result in the new exodus: "For the Lord will go before you, and the God of Israel will be your rear guard" (52:12). This means that when the sovereignty of God is near at hand one can, and indeed must, free himself or herself to meet it. In the messianic time the impossible becomes possible. The lordship of God makes it possible for human beings to be free. This understanding is also contained in Jesus' proclamation of the kingdom of God and in the apostle Paul's proclamation of Christ. The gospel announces the freeing lordship of God which belongs to the beginning of the messianic age. The gospel announces the eschatological exodus out of oppression into freedom. Only by way of conversion and change can the gospel be understood as good news.

For this reason the kingdom of God must first be preached to the "poor." They—and not the rich—are blessed (Luke 6:20). According to Matthew 11:28 the poor are those "who labor and are heavy laden." And according to Matthew 25:31 ff., those who are hungry, thirsty, imprisoned, and sick belong to the poor. The new creation of life for the whole world begins precisely with those who now exist on the edge of death. This is the proclamation of the gospel to the poor: a hopeless and unsaved people *(ochlos)* is called to become the messianic people *(laos)* of the coming Kingdom. The new creation begins on the "underside of society," and emancipation begins with the lowly.

Practical Consequences

A. Good news to the poor, healing the sick, justifying sinners—all of these appear *one-sided.* In a world divided into rich and poor, healthy and sick, good and bad, etc., the universalism of the kingdom of God can only be demonstrated through one-sided and clear identification with those who are exploited, despised and persecuted. Just as Jesus' mission to all humanity first took the form of a mission to the oppressed, so also the Christian community is present for everyone only when it is first present for the poor, the sick, the sinners. In a divided world, universalism and identification with a particular party or cause are not antithetical.

B. The freeing gospel liberates not through force and coercion, but through invitation and entreaty. "We beseech you on behalf of Christ, be reconciled to God" (II Cor. 5:20). "Come; for all is now ready" (Luke 14:17). Evangelizing must be freed therefore both from reliance on social pressure and apocalyptic threats of punishment in hell and an imminent catastrophic end of the world. Apocalyptic evangelizing robs the gospel of its liberating power and creates instead a faith grounded in anxiety. Evangelization is messianic rejoicing or it is no evangelization.

C. If the proclamation of the gospel is regarded as the exclusive province of ordained preachers and theologians, the whole enterprise becomes too authoritative and pretentious. As a result the congregation is silent. To be sure, Karl Barth described the Word of God as God's self-expression addressed to us. And Rudolf Bultmann spoke of kerygma as that which places a claim on every person and calls him or her to eschatological decision. But the core of the gospel is not just being addressed and being claimed; it is *telling a story.* If the messianic age begins with the announcement of the good news, then everyone must join in telling the story of this new future. The Four Gospels tell the story of Jesus as a history of his messianic mission. The Acts of the Apostles tell the story of the church of Jesus as an eschatological exodus story. The Christian community is a story-telling community: it tells the story of Jesus with bread and wine as the story of its hope "until he comes." It tells its own history of communion with Jesus—its history of suffering and its hope for history—and this is the way the church proclaims the gospel.

Baptism and our Christian Calling

Every change in theory demands a change in practice. Every change in practice requires a change in theory. Every change in theory and practice must bring a corresponding change in the rituals of life. One cannot easily piece together a new practice with an old theory. One can also not put together a new theory with an old ritual. All who are concerned about the future of the church seek the renewal of the church. All who out of their faith in Christ seek the renewal of the church want her to become genuinely the church of Jesus Christ. Therefore the religious rituals of the church must be examined for their legitimacy and believability. Do they bring the liberating will of Christ to expression or do they actually hinder that will?

If we look from this viewpoint at the practice and ritual of baptism, the baptism of infants becomes problematic. In order to analyze the nature of this problem, let us begin with an examination of its historical consequences, and then critique these consequences by measuring them against the biblical sources of the Christian faith.

The Historical Effects of Infant Baptism

Through the practice of infant baptism we have perpetuated an involuntary identification with the church from generation to generation. The baptism of children is the foundation stone of the state churches of Europe as it is of the civil religion we call Christendom. There is no possibility of creating a voluntary, independent, and mature community out of institutional churches to which people belong simply on the basis of being baptized as children. Only when the baptism of infants is replaced by baptism as a free response to the call of discipleship can there be reform which creates community in the church. Such a reformation cannot come without a new baptismal practice.

There are of course several traditional arguments for the baptism of infants such as the following:

1) Christian baptism of the newborn is an initiation rite like those found among many races and peoples. It corresponds to Jewish circumcision and represents the acceptance of the child into the community of the family and the wider religious community. A child is, as Thomas Aquinas said, "an entity from its father and at the same time

an extension and expansion of its father's personhood." For this reason the children of Christian parents are baptized and are taken into grace and the covenant family.

2) The baptism of small children demonstrates in an especially perceptible way the prevenience of God's grace and the fact that justification is based on grace alone. It is argued that the practice of baptizing children guards against every tendency toward Pelagianism. Grace is *ex opere operato* and is not dependent upon the faith either of the one baptized or the one baptizing.

3) Only in modern societies, it is claimed, have human beings developed a sense of purely individual consciousness. In every other society individual consciousness has as its context the collective consciousness of the family, the race, the people. Single individuals cannot convert and be baptized simply because there are no genuinely individual persons but only members of larger social units. Therefore the church must convert and baptize these larger collectives of family, tribes, and peoples. This has been indeed the traditional baptismal practice. When the chieftan or king was baptized then in principle the whole tribe or an entire kingdom was baptized. The practice of the baptism of infants has followed from this understanding. Before we consider these arguments further, however, let us ask what the Christian meaning of baptism is.

Baptism as a Sign of the Messianic Life

Christian baptism originated out of the baptismal movement of John the Baptist. Therefore it has nothing to do with an initiation rite. It also is not a substitute for the Hebrew rite of circumcision. The movement of John the Baptist was a prophetic call to repentence in the light of the coming judgment of God. The desert preacher called for a new Exodus. When he baptized in the Jordan this symbolized leaving slavery and servitude behind and entering into the promised land of God's sovereignty. Baptism was therefore an expression of radical change, of turning in a new direction. By anticipating the judgment of

God it guaranteed that one would be spared from that judgment in the end time. It was understood therefore as an eschatological sacrament of repentance.

Jesus' baptism by John the Baptist is one thing that is historically certain. Jesus began as John's disciple and stepped forward to initiate his own mission only after John was taken prisoner. Jesus himself did not baptize. Yet the community that came into existence at Easter began baptizing almost immediately. How can we explain this? The baptism of Jesus by John is an indication that Jesus took over John's eschatology of the imminent advent of the kingdom of God. The fact that Jesus separated himself from the circle of John the Baptist's disciples is an indication, however, that Jesus' own gospel of eschatological judgment differed from that of the Baptist. John had proclaimed the imminence of the kingdom of God in terms of judgment which calls forth repentence. Jesus proclaimed the imminence of the kingdom of God in terms of mercy through the forgiveness of sins which makes faith and trust in God possible. Therefore Jesus' disciples were not called upon to fast, and they did not go into the wilderness but into the villages. Their manner of living was not apocalyptic, but messianic. The community which came into existence after Easter soon baptized, and that baptism was "with the Holy Spirit." Their experiences of Easter were experiences of the Spirit, and these experiences of the Spirit were understood as first signs of the new creation in the midst of this world which is passing away. The eschatology of the earliest Christian community, therefore, went beyond the eschatology of the earthly Jesus. Baptism was for them an "eschatological sacrament of the Spirit" and is to be understood as *eschatology in practice;* it symbolized the inbreaking of the lordship of God over a human life. It was *hope in action;* it symbolized the beginning of the new creation of the world in the rebirth of a human being.

A more developed theology of baptism is found in Paul. According to Romans 6, the faithful are baptized into the death of Christ and through baptism are buried with him. In this fellowship with Christ they die to the powers of this world—sin, the law, and death—and are resurrected to new life with Christ. According to I Corinthians 12, the faithful are called with baptism into the charismatic community, and each person is given his or her own kind of service to do. Baptism demonstrates the new identity of the person in Christ; therefore a new name is given. It underscores each person as having a task in the history of the coming kingdom; each has a calling. It unites the life of the individual, which by itself would be insignificant, with the liberation and salvation of the whole cosmos; therefore baptism gives a certainty of meaning to life.

In short, the Christian meaning of baptism contradicts the practice of infant baptism and invalidates each of the arguments previously given:

1) Baptism is in its very nature not an initiation rite but an eschatological sign of the Holy Spirit which presupposes faith and hope.

2) Even the signs of prevenient grace are directed toward faith and have faith as their object. Only for faith can we say that baptism works *ex opere operato* or *verbo vocante*. Even the baptism of infants assumes faith, namely the faith of parents, sponsors, and the church. The infants of non-Christians have never been baptized.

3) While collective consciousness is just as important as individual consciousness, it should be grounded not in tribal baptism or infant baptism, but only in the corporate responsibility of the baptized for their nation, their people, and their children.

Baptism and Calling:
Suggestions for a New Baptismal Practice

The kind of baptism which corresponds to the Christian meaning of baptism is baptism as *incorporation into the Christian calling to discipleship and service.*

A. What ought to happen to the newborn children of Christians is not their baptism but rather the calling of the parents, the sponsors, and the Christian community to the Christian nurture of the children. For with the advent of a child comes a new charism, the gift of the parenthood. The appropriate liturgical celebration of this is the blessing of the child which should include calling upon the parents and sponsors to exercise the new charism entrusted to them.

B. From this call addressed to the parents, the sponsors, and the congregation to nurture children follows the task of incorporating the children into the story of the gospel, that is, to instruct them in their basic identity as part of the community. At the end of the process of instruction in the story of the gospel should come the question of personal acceptance of the call into fellowship with Christ and service of the kingdom of God.

C. The baptism which follows should not be regarded as "believer's baptism." To be sure, it happens on the basis of faith. However, it is not feelings of faith or experiences of conversion which are to be testified to through baptism, but the *calling* into which the person has entered. Therefore I suggest the expression "baptism into Christian calling" *(Berufungstaufe)*.

D. For the individual, baptism means the public confession of one's new identity in Christ (Col. 3:3) and, as a result, freedom toward all other identifications and loyalties. It means further the public expression of one's integration into the history of the kingdom of God, that is, into the messianic liberation of the world. Baptism testifies that finite life has found an infinite meaning.

E. Without a new *fellowship community* this way of discipleship is not possible. The baptized person needs a group which undergirds and supports his or her existence. Only to the degree that the church is able to move from an uncommitted civil religion to a recognizable fellowship in the messianic history of God can the baptism into discipleship be realized. At the same time, the church will only become a community in this sense through a transition from the involuntary baptism of infants to the liberating baptism of disciples. There can be no genuine church reform without the reform of baptismal practices. At the same time, there can be no genuine reform of baptism without reform of the church.

The Eschatological Eucharist:
Eating and Drinking in the Kingdom of God

If the future of the church lies with the renewal of local congregations, then the community and fellowship of the Lord's Supper must move to the center of the services and assemblies of the congregation. For fellowship in eating and drinking at the table of the Lord constitutes the genuine life together of the community. In times of persecution and oppression in the history of Protestantism, the Lord's Supper has always come to the fore. In times of ease and security, the Lord's Supper has always been neglected. This indicates how much the Lord's Supper strengthens the congregation for resistance. Therefore, in all denominations we need a consistent Christianizing of the sacrament in order that it can no longer be misunderstood in a ritualistic or magical way. Out of its biblical origins this eschatological meal of joy gives human beings in exile the strength to resist and the energy of the Holy Spirit.

The Fellowship Meal and the Church's Divisions

The Lord's Supper is in its very essence a fellowship meal. The churches have split, however, over differences in its theory and practice, and so today we celebrate the Orthodox "eucharist," the Catholic "mass" and the Protestant "communion." The ecumenical healing of the conflicts between the churches began with a new understanding of the meal as the supper of the Lord. As the Lord's Supper it is first of all Christ's meal, and only then the meal of the church. This means that to this meal the Lord himself invites his own. No church has the right to restrict his invitation or set conditions. His invitation to the meal is just as open and as universal as his sacrifice "for many" on Golgotha. His hands which invite to the table are the outstretched hands of the Crucified One. The only qualification for acceptance of this open invitation is that we recognize the Giver of the feast. Things such as "pure doctrine," church discipline, and recognition of church authorities cannot be coupled with the invitation to the meal if one recognizes that Christ himself is the host. Dogmatic, moral, and clerical legalisms destroy not only the gospel but also the appetite. At this table what comes first is the eating—and then come morality, dogmatics, and ecclesiastical order. First comes the experience of fellowship with Christ and fellowship with one another, and then comes a common theory concerning this experience. To be sure, there are in the ecumenical movement three different understandings of the point at which table fellowship can occur. For the Orthodox churches the eucharist stands at the end of the ecumenical movement as its goal and crown. For the Roman Catholics, the condition for the eucharist is the recognition of the universal authority of the pope. Most Protestant churches favor the unconditional recognition of the open invitation of Christ.

The Gospel and the Banquet of the Kingdom of God

What is the original meaning of this meal? If Jesus announced the "good news of the kingdom of God," then according to the prophetic hope he must also anticipate eating and drinking in the kingdom of God. When he announced the Kingdom to "the poor" he ate and drank with sinners and publicans, for the good news of the messianic age is inseparably bound together with the messianic meal. According to Isaiah 25, the kingdom of God is that great banquet of joy in Zion for all nations. According to Matthew 8:11 and Luke 13:29, they will come "from east and west, and from north and south, and sit at table in the kingdom of God." The parable of the great wedding feast (Matthew 22:2-10) shows how human liberation is identified with the fellowship meal in the kingdom of God. The meal is the "materialism" of God's kingdom. Therefore *the table fellowship of Jesus with the poor, those without rights, and sinners* is to be understood as Jesus anticipating the banquet of the justified in the kingdom of God. Jesus opens up the Kingdom by forgiving sins and by eating and drinking with sinners (Luke 15:2). The *meals of Jesus with his disciples* are also to be understood within this messianic context. This is seen in his words at the Last Supper. "For I tell you that from now on I shall not drink of the fruit of the vine until the kingdom of God comes" (Luke 22:18). Jesus' meals with his disciples were not exclusive meals of the righteous or the elect, but rather meals of the friends of Jesus who participate in his mission "to seek and to save the lost" (Luke 19:10). So from the beginning fellowship with Jesus and participation in the kingdom of God were identified with table fellowship. The kingdom of God is not only announced and believed, but also eaten and drunk.

The *Last Supper* of Jesus with his disciples before his death has always had a special meaning for the Christian community (I Cor. 11). For this meal was characterized as the gift of Jesus' own life and blood "for many." It made the kingdom of God present not in the direct way that Jesus did in his own table fellowship, but as mediated through the self-giving of Christ. While being the giver of the meal, Jesus is himself the gift. He is the gift of the kingdom of God in his very person. Through his bodily self-giving for many he brought the kingdom of God to the godless. Therefore we receive the kingdom of God as the life and blood of Christ in the form of bread and wine.

One must recognize this concentration of the kingdom of God in the person and death of Jesus in order to grasp why christology and eschatology come to focus in the paschal meal. Through this meal the death of Christ is to be remembered until he comes (I Cor. 11:26). In the presence of the Resurrected One, Jesus' self-giving to the point of death on the cross is recalled. In his sacrificial death on the cross the kingdom of God is promised. Eschatological hope is celebrated in the power of this memory. Communion with Christ is "eating and drinking in the kingdom of God," and eating and drinking in the kingdom of God are communion with Christ. As an eating and drinking in remembrance of Christ's promises, this meal is eating and drinking unto hope.

Christian table fellowship includes in itself therefore: (1) The last meal of Jesus with his disciples which anticipated his death on the cross, (2) the table fellowship of Jesus with the poor, and with sinners and publicans, and (3) the prophetic hope for the great banquet of all peoples in Zion.

In the light of these three factors the meal must certainly be an open one.

Practical Suggestions for Open Communion

A. There should be no congregational assemblies for worship without table fellowship, no proclamation of the gospel of the Kingdom without eating and drinking in the Kingdom with Jesus! The meal belongs in the center of the worship. Worship must be celebrated with bread and wine. The church becomes a genuine fellowship through eating and drinking together, and the fellowship meal demands that the church be a genuine community.

B. The fellowship around the table must be open fellowship: (1) open to all disciples of Christ regardless of denomination and (2) open to "publicans and sinners." The only condition which can be set is that we be clear that in this meal we have to do with the Jesus who is crucified for us and that in this meal the kingdom of God stands open to us.

C. The celebration of the Lord's Supper ought to be combined with an Agape meal, for bread and wine are not earthly symbols of a heavenly event, but a foretaste of the feeding of all humankind in the kingdom of God. Between the Lord's Supper and the great banquet of the nations lies the hunger of the world. The eucharist makes us keenly aware of the injustice of hunger and makes that injustice insufferable. An Agape meal is not just a love feast attached to a ritual meal, but a shalom meal which demonstrates the eschatological hope for overcoming the hunger of the world. As a meal open to the whole church, the Lord's Supper demonstrates the catholicity of the local congregation. As a meal open to the world for "publicans and sinners," it demonstrates the messianic mission of the congregation. As a meal open to the future and to the hungry and thirsty, it demonstrates the hope of the congregation for the kingdom of God.

In summary, therefore, the future of the church lies with the renewal of the local church. The renewal of the local church waits upon the renewal of the forms and practices by which we express our common life together. And the renewal of forms and practices is dependent upon seeing the whole life of the church—indeed, the whole life of the world—in the context of the coming kingdom of God. The biblical message of the Kingdom relativizes time-honored traditions and familiar practices, and enables us to grasp the new possibilities for praxis that are inherent in the gospel. This is the freeing power of the kingdom as it applies to the life of the church.

Moltmann's Contribution to Practical Theology
M. Douglas Meeks

Among the major systematic theologians today none goes further to meet the practical theologian on common ground and in a common task than does Jürgen Moltmann. Indeed, his definition of theology as the theory of the practice of the church allies him from the beginning with those who want to see theology carried on in responsibility to the life and mission of the church without, of course, compromising the independence and critical role of theology.

One might anticipate that a theologian for whom eschatology is so important would exalt the prophetic role of preaching as the main function of ministry. Such an emphasis on one aspect of ministry to the exclusion of others is readily visible in the past history of the church. Gregory the Great, for example, considered "ruling" or governing the Christian community to be the principal pastoral function. Preaching, teaching, and other duties were understood in this light. The concept of the pastor as ruler shaped the medieval view of the clergy and the character of the church.[1] The churches of the Reformation raised preaching to a preeminent position and subordinated other aspects of the church's life. Today pastoral care and counseling appear to have been installed as an exhaustive model of ministry by many clergy and their parishioners.

For Moltmann, however, no one aspect of ministry has the right to preeminence over the others because their relationship is essentially complementary. Each is necessary to the others for the wholeness of the church and its calling in the world. The holistic approach has two sources in Moltmann's theology. Most basically it is grounded in his doctrine of the Trinity, in which he argues for the complementarity of the Persons of the Trinity and against the reductionism and practical unitarianism which infiltrate the church and popular religion when one or another of the Persons becomes dominant and the others are subordinated or neglected.[2]

The second source of Moltmann's holistic approach to ministry is in his understanding of the church as a "charismatic community," i.e., as a fellowship in which the gifts for ministry are distributed to *all* the members (Rom. 12; I Cor. 12) and in which no one is to consider oneself or one's gifts as superior to others. Because each person is gifted by the Holy Spirit, each person is called to ministry in and through the Body of Christ.[3] Thus Moltmann offers a corrective to our habitual tendency, visible throughout the history of the church, to think of ministry in terms of the functions of the professional clergy rather than the ministries exercised by the whole people of God.

Models for Practical Theology

In order better to understand Moltmann's contribution it will be helpful to compare his position with the models of practical theology currently in vogue.

Howard Grimes has summarized three models in describing the relation of practical theology to its sources.[4] The first model, which Grimes identifies with Karl Barth, sees practical theology growing out of systematic theology. Edward Thurneysen's *A Theology of Pastoral Care* is a chief example of this approach which was followed extensively in American theological schools in the 40s and 50s.[5] For Barth, theology is the discipline which compares the actually existing church with the proclamation of the Word which is the foundation of the church's practice.[6] All decisions and actions in the church not only live out of the Word but must also be critically examined for their truth by the Word. Thus practical theology, as well as ethics, involves the central task of searching for the truth and faithfulness of the church in the Word of God. Practical theology of course represents distinct questions which require unique methods of reflection and action, but these methods are grounded in the overall framework of church dogmatics. For Barth, if any one discipline goes its own way, it falls outside the examination of the whole of the church's practice according to the Word of God. It then becomes an unexamined channel for definitions of authority which are not appropriate to the Word of God. This approach to practical theology tends to narrow the understanding of church practice to the act of proclamation.

Grimes associates the second model with the recent emphasis on the human sciences—psychology and sociology—in American theological education and names Seward Hiltner as a chief proponent.[7] This approach reflects the widespread loss of confidence in systematic, biblical, and historical theology in our century (although in many instances it utilizes extreme existentialist theologies of freedom and justification, theologies which burned themselves out and left an empty space in which practical theology could be done without theological assumptions). This model assumes that the form for practical theology is best derived from the human sciences and that its content comes from "theological reflection upon pastoral operations seen from the shepherding perspective."[8] This model does not question current forms and practices of professional ministry from a theological perspective, but asks how we can do what we are already doing more effectively and scientifically. A normative function is assigned to the human sciences—especially psychology and psychotherapy—and the effectiveness of ministry is judged from a psychological point of view. As a result, this approach tends to reduce practical theology to pastoral care and pastoral care to counseling. This means that proclamation, evangelization, Christian education, communal discipline, and mission in the world tend to be neglected because they are seen as less important elements in the praxis of professional ministry.

We might pause here to observe that the first two models could be, and indeed have often been, called *pastoral* theology instead of *practical* theology because they tend to identify ministry with the professional clergy. To be sure, in the first model the pastor's work is defined by the internal life of the church, whereas in the second model the professional minister may understand himself or herself in terms of the medico-psychological role of secular disciplines. But in both models we are still under the pale of Gregory: the pastor or the professional minister is the undisputed ruler, the leader of a "flock," or a clientele, who are the object of his preaching or care.

The third model understands the task of practical theology to be to juxtapose systematic theology and the human situation. If the approach of the first model was deductive, and that of the second was inductive, the approach of the third is lateral. This view of practical theology follows Tillich's method of correlation. Sometimes the starting point is systematic theology; at other times the secular sciences are used to reflect on the cultural situation of the church.[9] The disciplines interact and influence one another, and none of them is considered an exclusive norm.

This approach to practical theology has given rise to much experimentation with new forms of worship, liturgy, community formation, and church administration. Any one of these functions may be the principal one around which practical theology is organized. In dialogue with the best scientific analyses and cultural statements, this method has resulted in the notion of a church which is open both to its tradition and to the world around it.

But in the end this method of correlation or juxtaposition is confusing because its openness and lack of norms mean that the rightful contributions of the human sciences often are not integrated in dialectical fashion within a clear theological context. Thus this approach tends to reinforce the present situation in many American churches, which exist with neither a center nor a horizon. This approach of practical theology often results in, even if it does not always intend to do so, the general accommodation and assimilation of our churches to the surrounding culture. Such secularization corresponds to the widespread inability of our churches to ask the question of truth regarding their faith or to have any authentic transforming impact on our society and culture.

Moltmann's Contribution to Defining Practical Theology

Now let us find out how Moltmann's theology offers a new model for understanding practical theology as over against the three paradigms just outlined. Moltmann's theology is preeminently a trinitarian theology which provides a consistent trinitarian view of the church. Practical theology is ultimately determined by the view of the church which it takes as normative. For Moltmann, the church is understood as a function of God's trinitarian history with the world. The church is part of God's history, his suffering, his yearning, his acting for the liberation and reconciliation of his whole creation. The Trinity is God's own being in action. The creating Father, the reconciling Son, and the sanctifying Spirit are equally important and necessary aspects of the one divine event of God in the world. According to Moltmann, therefore, each and every form of practice in the church is a function of God's trinitarian history, and the equality of the Persons is the basis for the equality of the various ministries, or charismata, in the church. This means that no one form of ministry can be considered more important than the others. At no time, for example, should preaching and teaching or pastoral care or service to the world be considered the exclusive model or form of the church's ministry, even though we will always be tempted to emphasize one in order to redress imbalances. Rather, all questions of practice should be determined by the trinitarian history of which the church is only a part, only an instrument.

I believe that Moltmann's main contribution to practical theology is that he places it in a trinitarian context. And I say this with two of his formidable predecessors in mind, Friedrich Schleiermacher and Karl Barth. The modern discipline of practical theology originated with Schleiermacher, who viewed all of theology as a function of the church. Practical theology is the crown of theology because the practical field is the one where all theology is put to work in the service of the church.[10]

Schleiermacher is right. Everything practical theology does *should* be done as a function of the church and in the service of the church. Occasionally in this century certain branches of theology, including practical theology, have gone off on their own and assumed that they could do their own thing, irrespective of the church. When this happens, we must be reminded that theology is a function of the church and is thus accountable to the church.

But this is only the first step, and if we hold only to this step we will fall into the extreme danger that all forms of theology, including practical theology, become nothing but the ideology of church practice and practical theologians nothing but functionaries of the church.

Karl Barth has made the next necessary point better than anyone else. He went along with his old nemesis, Schleiermacher, in assuming that all theology will be church theology, but Barth's chief point was that practical theology is not merely a function of the church precisely because the church is a function of the ministry and lordship of Jesus Christ. The church is not the first word of God. Jesus Christ is God's first word. The church belongs to Jesus Christ. It speaks and lives and acts in his name and no other. Thus all practice, every decision, action, and structure of the church must be referred to the lordship of Jesus Christ. There is nothing in the church, not even the finance committee meeting, which does not have to be referred to the authority of the church's Author!

But this second step in understanding practical theology can also be dangerous. If we stop here we will tend to view everything in terms of Jesus Christ and the church, and we too quickly get the idea that the church as the proclaimer of Christ is authorized to be the last word of God without even considering what God is doing and will do with the rest of his creation.

It is here that Moltmann makes his contribution. He agrees that practical theology is a function of the church and that the church is a function of Jesus Christ, but we must go on to say that Jesus Christ is a function of the ultimate lordship of God. Jesus Christ proclaims the coming kingdom of God. And the messianic community which Christ calls into being proclaims Christ and his suffering, reconciling love, as the way into that Kingdom. When the Kingdom comes in its ultimacy the church will be superfluous; it will no longer be needed. God's glory and beauty and creative joy will penetrate everything that is. In the meantime, however, the church is an instrument, an all-important part of God's own redemptive history. And in this fact we are provided the profoundest basis and the broadest horizon for practical theology. What new ways can we begin to think of practical theology and church practice in view of their context in the trinitarian history of God with the world?

If we want to give an overall term to Moltmann's theology, I think we could call it a theology of reconciliation and mediation. At every juncture Moltmann's theology is trying to put together what in theology and church practice have often been torn asunder. The mediating element is the crucial consideration. God's own life and activity as Father, Son, and Holy Spirit is, according to Moltmann, one of constant mediation within himself and in his relation to the world. God does not work in monotheistic, monolithic, imperial, and totalitarian ways. God is not a simple being, nor simply being. Nor does God work in dualistic, dichotomous, and two-kingdom ways. God is not divided against himself in simple polarities or dialectics. God is trinitarian, and he works in trinitarian ways for reconciliation. Now let us see how this structure is evident in Moltmann's theology.

I want to suggest that each of Moltmann's three major books represents an approach to one aspect of God's trinitarian history and that each aspect requires the others. Moltmann relates each in turn to a particular function of the church, and each of these functions requires the others in order for the church to be the church in its fullness. *Theology of Hope* focuses on the resurrection, *The Crucified God* on the life and cross of Jesus, and *The Church in the Power of the Spirit* on Pentecost. But each book, although focused on one event of the trinitarian history of God, implicates the other two.

In *Theology of Hope* everything is put in an eschatological key. We look at everything from the perspective of the Father, the future of God, hope, and mission. The corresponding function of the church is diakonia, the self-giving of the church in service of the kingdom of God in the world. In *The Crucified God* everything is put in a christological, historical key. We look at everything from the perspective of the Son, the at-handness of God's rule of righteousness, faith, and the liberated and liberating church. The corresponding function of the church is kerygma, the proclamation of promise and freedom in the gospel. In *The Church in the Power of the Spirit* everything is put in a pneumatological key. We look at everything from the perspective of the Holy Spirit, the historical empowerment of the church, love, and the charismatic congregation. The corresponding function of the church is koinonia, the creation and formation of the new humanity of Jesus Christ in the Spirit.

If there is a fundamental thesis in Moltmann's theology it is that all three of these aspects belong together in God's trinitarian history with the world. On the level of knowing, they interpret each other. On the level of being, they are constitutive of each other. One does not exist without the other two. The resulting fundamental thesis for practical theology would be, I believe, that all the functions of the church—proclamation, community, and service—belong together. Each interprets the others. Each is a precondition for the others, and each is constitutive for the others. To realize this in theory and practice has vast implications for practical theology and church life.

Moltmann's theology of the church would not totally discard the three prevalent models mentioned earlier. In fact elements from each are taken up in Moltmann's theology. The Word of God, the experience of the church interpreted in terms of the social sciences, and the world-openness of the church all appear in Moltmann's theology. Yet these are not self-constituting. Instead each is related to God's trinitarian dealing with the world.

Theology of Hope and the Missionary Church

In one sense Moltmann's theology of the church develops out of the general Barthian and Reformation approach. He believes with Calvin and Barth that the church is the *creatura verbi,* the creature of the Word. But in his first book which captured world-wide attention, *Theology of Hope,* Moltmann demonstrated that the original strength of the Reformation's emphasis on Word and faith leading to justification has in the present become a weakness. In protecting this Protestant fortress composed of Word, faith, and justification, modern Protestant theology has paid little attention to promise, hope, the future, and the mission of the church in the world. In the first stage of his theology Moltmann sought to show that according to the biblical traditions God does not reveal himself to those who have faith by immediately disclosing the presence of his being in such a way that history is in effect completed. Rather, argued Moltmann, the Word of God has the structure of a promise.[11] Faith in the Word of God looks not only for the revelation of God and his name but also for the realization of God's promises.

This means that Christian faith always gives rise to hope. Or rather hope in God's promises makes faith historical; it makes faith look and yearn for what God is yet to do in his promised future. God's defeat of death in the resurrection of the crucified Jesus is the beginning of faith, and God's promise in the resurrection that he will defeat death in us and in all things makes us live in the mode of hope. Thus Christians exist "between the times," between God's raising of Jesus from the dead and his promised defeat of death in all things. Christians live in history in the modes of hope, faith, and love, not depending on any securities of history or nature or human artifact, but on God's faithfulness to himself and his word of promise. That is the meaning of the historical existence to which God calls us.

Over against the general Reformation and Barthian theology of the church, Moltmann's theology has the effect of opening up the church to history and to the world. It is missionary and ecumenical theology. A preaching church which produces justified people is not enough. Nor is a closed-community church which supplies people with "warm fuzzies" to compensate for the cold, objectified world they live in. Rather, the church has to be understood as the missionary church through and through. The church is mission. Moltmann views the resurrection appearances as essentially calling and sending appearances.[12] In them the risen Christ, on the basis of God's own promise, commissions the church to be in mission. The resurrection is a history-making event, it is God's creation of that peculiar history in which Christians are called to witness to Jesus until the final verdict about him is in. Before it was anything, the church was sent into mission. Thus the mission does not arise from the church; rather the mission of Christ created and creates the church. Mission comprehends the whole of the church, not merely parts of it. It does not refer simply to those who are sent out; it refers to what brings the church into existence in the first place and its continuing raison d'être.

In *Theology of Hope* Moltmann developed an ecclesiology of the exodus church, the church which is on the move in history, not tied down to any place in the sense of class, race, or nation, but moving through them all announcing the open future of God's coming righteousness.[13] It is an ecclesiology which can speak to the only kind of atheism that ought to be taken seriously in the modern world—the atheism which disbelieves God for the sake of oppressed and humiliated human beings, an atheism which suffers with the whole enslaved world and yearns for freedom, and wonders why the church often has as its only reference—itself. The theology of the exodus church can be in dialogue with such atheism because it remembers Abraham, the father of our faith, who set out from Haran leaving kindred, property, nation, and security behind. More important, he left behind his father's household gods and thus became in the eyes of his own time an atheist, going through history, following nothing but the promise given to him. And it remembers Moses who, though the description of God he received from the burning bush scarcely qualified as a full-blown ontology, accepted the assignment to liberate his people and persisted merely with the assurance that in the midst of obedience to the mission and the task he would find out who God is.

The theology of the exodus church calls into question any practical theology which would draw narrow lines around the church, which would think of the church as an end in itself or as closed to the world. For Moltmann the mission of God mediates between history and eschatology. Practical theology should not speak in dualistic terms of the visible and the invisible church, the ideal and the real church, time and eternity, the church and the world. Practical theology should begin with the actually existing church. The churches that exist before our eyes are the only church we have. At the same time, everything in practical theology should be related to the church's mission in the ultimate horizon of God's kingdom. To carry out its mission the church must constantly negotiate between that ultimate horizon and its concrete present situation, never losing sight of the one or the other.

However necessary and crucial the proclamation of the Word is, therefore, it cannot be understood as the exhaustive model for practical theology. Proclamation of God's promise and of freedom in Christ serves evangelization, and evangelization serves mission, and mission embraces all activities that serve to liberate human beings from their slavery in the presence of the coming God, whether that slavery is economic, political, cultural, or personal. The simple fact is that the church is not here to serve itself. It is here to serve God's eschatological Word which is his ultimate redemption of all things. Thus every facet of church practice is meant to call the church and the world into full participation in the mission of God himself as he moves toward the ultimate defeat of sin, death, and evil.

The theology of hope sees revelation, Jesus, and the church from the perspective of God's eschatological rule. But the theology of hope has been misunderstood by many Christians. Many North Americans, for example, took it merely as a new sophisticated rationale for American optimism, for futurological and utopian thinking, for the open future of the *homo Americanus* and the American way of life, and as a theology reflecting the notion that all things are possible in the church and through its activity in the world. This is a careless reading of *Theology of Hope*, to say the least. Such a reading does not see that at the heart of the theology of hope is the proclamation of the cross and the Crucified One. The theology of hope is not a *theologia gloriae*. It concentrates on one aspect of God's trinitarian dealings with the world, but only as that aspect is conjoined with the other two. It is an emphasis on resurrection, exodus, the eschaton, hope, historical anticipation, and mission. But not to the exclusion of other factors.

The Crucified God and the Political Church under the Cross

Moltmann's next major book, *The Crucified God*, turned from the emphasis on the future *horizon* of Christian faith to the *center* of Christian faith. As an attempt to reinterpret the Reformation doctrine of justification in terms of liberation, it does not contradict *Theology of Hope*, but it does call into question any facile, over-simplified views. It questions, for example, the optimistic, futuristic views of our liberal churches. What good is the assurance of an open future to people who are sick, in despair, and dying today? What good is a theory of mission if there is no real freedom which enables people to enter into mission? What does the church gain if it incorporates the world's promises into itself without asking whether those promises are actually freeing promises?

So without laying aside the emphasis on hope and God's kingdom, Moltmann moved to his next question: How is the power of the resurrection—God's power to create life in his ultimate rule—already mediated in this world under the conditions of history? The answer *The Crucified God* gives is that God's ultimate liberation comes into history through God's suffering. We are shown the coming kingdom of God from the perspective of Jesus' announcement of the Kingdom at hand. We see the resurrection from the perspective of the passion and crucifixion of Jesus. We look at the mission of the church in the world from the perspective of God's justifying us in Jesus Christ. We view energizing hope from the perspective of liberating faith. When we ask who God is and what he is doing in the world, we have to tell the history of Israel and the story of Jesus Christ. This means that at the center of church praxis is God's messianic history of liberation and suffering.

The ecclesiology that Moltmann developed in *The Crucified God* is that of a *liberated* and *liberating* church, a *political* church. By "political" Moltmann does not mean that we are to politicize the church in the sense of declaring it a part of this political party or that, or by insisting that it should announce one political manifesto after another. Rather he claims that the church is always and necessarily political not only because it lives in the world but because of the gospel it proclaims. Whenever the gospel of God's messianic freedom in Jesus Christ is proclaimed it causes power conflicts. Liberating faith has to do with judging all claims to power in terms of the affirmation of Christ's lordship over everything. In this sense the gospel is political. If it is believed and lived it causes contradictions, struggles, and resistance. The power which liberates takes the shape of the cross, and it is bound to cause conflicts with other claims to power in the world. Every claim to power must be tested as to its real ability to free human beings in terms of the ultimate source of freedom—the cross of Jesus Christ.

This is the reason I believe that the social science model of practical theology, which is surely one of the most widespread in American theological schools and church practice, should be called into question.[14] This model, which is heavily dependent upon human and social sciences, tends to narrow Christian ministry and church life to pastoral care and psychological liberation. This model of practical theology has risen to its place of extreme importance for a number of reasons. First, there has been in this century a growing loss of confidence, and often for good reasons, in confessional, creedal, and biblical theology. In its most extreme form this is a loss of faith that the gospel has the power to free human beings. Second, there has been a retreat of the modern church from the contradictions and antagonisms of economics, politics, and culture. More and more the church has struck a compromise with the existing economic system, the university, the courthouse, and the legislature to the effect that the human, social, economic, political, and natural sciences may take charge of the public and natural world so that eventually the church will be left with only the private, internal world of the individual, because it fails to witness to the lordship of Jesus Christ over every dimension of life in the world. Furthermore, and this is a third reason, the lordship of Jesus Christ no longer extends even to the private, internal life as the church puts more and more confidence in the methods of psychotherapeutic theories to free people. A fourth reason may be that we clergy have felt more and more defensive about our profession in a contemporary society which measures everything by standards of production, consumption, and success. Consequently we are tempted to borrow from psychological and social sciences a certain dignity of professional standing. For all or any one of these reasons many clergy and laity today understand that which is of central significance in the church almost completely in terms of pastoral care and counseling.

For similar reasons other clergy understand the life and practice of the church almost exclusively in terms of administration. They call on the social sciences of cybernetics and organizational development and tend to assume that ministry is basically a matter of internally shaping the church according to the best organizational models available in our society.

The church and theological education are slowly beginning to wake up and realize that the uncritical enthusiasm with which they have taken over every new fad and trend in the human and social sciences is self-defeating. The political church under the cross will certainly be open to using resources offered by the human and social sciences when it can be determined that such methods are indeed liberating according to the gospel's criteria. But it will not enthusiastically and blindly accept whatever comes its way. In its search after anything and everything that will satisfy its urge for the novel and the relevant, the church today occasionally looks like a camel in heat! Although this is a biblical image, I don't think it is a biblical model for the church.

Pastoral therapy has developed into a sophisticated field of its own and has made, to be sure, tremendous contributions. But when it incorporates psychotherapeutic theories and methods into the church without critically scrutinizing the cultural and social assumptions connected with them, such a practice is not serving the freedom of the church in Christ. Pastoral counseling often deals with the emotional and psychological problems of individuals without touching the larger social, cultural, political, and economic assumptions that have in the first place contributed to their emotional disorder. Recently pastoral counseling has been practiced more and more outside the church altogether, which not only robs pastoral care of the resources of the gathered people of God, but also intensifies the ominous trend toward privatism in our society. I am not denying the place and necessity of therapy in the practice of ministry, but I am questioning whether therapeutic theories can provide the models for practical theology and the practice of ministry.

In similar ways, practical theology that is built around church administration often merely imports the most successful theories of the multinational corporations without being critical of the values and the assumptions about society and human beings that come with these theories. A political church committed to God's messianic history of liberation is not opposed to organization and institution; But it knows that it will have to test every theory of organization by the form of the cross, lest its own organizational structure merely reflect and confirm the unjust institutions of our society.

The Power of the Spirit and the Charismatic Congregation

Now we turn to the third aspect in Moltmann's trinitarian understanding of the church. If we have a theory of the church as mission in the world and a theory of mediation through God's freedom and power to create life in the world through his suffering, what more do we need? The answer is the mature congregation created by the Holy Spirit. Missionary theologies and liberation theologies need an actual historical agent to carry out their theories—or they remain only theories. Moltmann's third major book, *The Church in the Power of the Spirit,* focuses on the power out of which the church can actually be formed in the world. In this book Moltmann explores the concept which the mainline Reformers used polemically against the Medieval church but which they never fully realized, namely, the "congregation." The congregation, as it is created and formed by God the Holy Spirit, is placed in the world to mediate God's righteousness and freedom. Everything depends therefore on the formation of a genuinely charismatic congregation. By "charismatic" Moltmann means the apostle Paul's conception that everything in the church begins with the Holy Spirit's gifting of each person with the "charismata," the gifts of ministry. Because each person is gifted and empowered by the Holy Spirit, each person has a ministry and is a minister.[15] Where the Spirit is active there will be experimentation and innovation. Diaconal groups will emerge, and there will be counter movements within and without the church, groups that yearn for the breath of the Spirit within a dead and stultifying church. Moltmann's theology moves away from the overclericalized, pastoral church toward the church of the whole people of God. It is a theology which takes sanctification seriously and emphasizes that faith has to be actually experienced and expressed in a life-style that has a form and a discipline: a messianic life-style of fellowship.

Now I want to contrast this aspect of Moltmann's trinitarian theology of the church with the third model of practical theology suggested earlier: correlation/juxtaposition. When we juxtapose theology and the world we either remain ideal and theoretical in our practice or, as is more often the case, we end up depending on the signs of the time to determine the next step of practice. To be sure, this process gives a certain flexibility to the church, but then church practice is determined by the needs of the culture and society. "The world sets the agenda."

This model has led in the last two decades to a new sensitivity to all sorts of ministries in the world, even to dropping out of the church altogether to engage in "secular ministries." As theological seminaries developed courses in a variety of specialized ministries to meet those needs, we turned out people who were skilled in almost everything but the formation of the congregation. It should now be clear to us that the malaise in the church as a whole is in large part due to this widespread failure actually to form and nurture congregations out of the presence and power of the Holy Spirit. We can point to failures in the large churches, in the national boards and agencies, and in the ecumenical movements which have produced beautiful programs only to find that there is nobody there to carry them out. Many pastors have become disillusioned and disappointed because programs and forms of administration on the local level do not succeed in bringing the congregation to life. The split between clergy and laity has grown with the increased professionization of ministry. So-called charismatic renewal groups often tear persons away from the church into an escapist life-style that does not bring authentic renewal but provides spiritual reinforcement for the dehumanizing economic and political conditions in our society.

The only answer to this malaise is the genuinely charismatic congregation. The true charismatic fellowship is the radical beginning point for ecclesiology and practical theology in our day. It has the potential to break down and reconcile the deadening dualisms that separate liberals and conservatives, spiritualists and political activists, clergy and laity, the church as ministerial, hierarchical rule and the church as community. The charismatic congregation is called to be nothing less than the mediator of God's liberating history to the world. I believe this discovery in our midst can mean the dawning of new and incredibly exciting days for practical theology and the practice of ministry in the church.

Practicing Theology Between God's History of Liberation and the Charismatic Congregation

To summarize, the emerging definition of the nature and task of practical theology from the perspective of Moltmann's theology can be made in three points. In a sense everything in the church begins with the proclamation of the gospel. But if the church exists in the trinitarian history of God, this fact does not lead to an exclusively preaching church. Preaching, teaching, and evangelism must be intimately related to the functions of koinonia and diakonia. Proclamation of the promise and the freedom of the gospel leads to the creation of the new humanity in communion with Jesus and to service in the world—or the good news has not yet happened. It is the task of practical theology to make certain that this happens.

In a sense everything in the church depends on the formation of the charismatic congregation. However, if the church exists in the trinitarian history of God, this fact will not lead to an exclusively community-building church. Liturgy, pastoral care, and ministries and offices must be intimately related to the function of kerygma and diakonia. The charismatic congregation remembers and tells the story of Jesus, is freed to the interests of Christ, and gives itself to the world—or it has not yet come into being. It is the task of practical theology to make certain that this happens.

In a sense everything in the church is aimed at the actual gathering and sending out of the messianic fellowship in service for the kingdom of God in the world. But if the church exists in the trinitarian history of God, this fact will not lead to an exclusively social action or religious welfare-church. Church administration, polity, ethics, and missiology must be intimately related to kerygma and koinonia. The mission of the church comes to life in the freedom of the gospel and the power of the inspirited community—or it has not yet begun. It is the task of practical theology to make certain that this happens.

Moltmann's Theology of the Cross and the Dilemma of Contemporary Pastoral Care
Rodney J. Hunter

Paul W. Pruyser, an eminent clinical psychologist at the Menninger Foundation in Topeka, Kansas, recently published a little book entitled *The Minister as Diagnostician*. A committed churchman, Pruyser expresses surprise, and not a little concern, that ministers and theological students doing pastoral training in his institution have seemed so little inclined to talk with patients or parishioners about faith, God, or religion—or even to think about their ministries in religious or theological terms. Instead, says Pruyser, "they manifested, and sometimes professed, that their basic theological disciplines were of little help to them in ordering their observations and planning their meliorative moves." Pruyser goes on:

They did not quite trust their parishioners' occasional use of theological language and their presentation of theological conflicts. Issues of faith were quickly "pulled" into issues of marital role behavior, adolescent protest against parents, or dynamics of transference in the counseling situation. There seemed to be an implicit suspicion of the relevance of theology, both to any client's life and to the method and content of the pastor's counseling process.[1]

"It is a jarring note," he concludes, "when any professional person no longer knows what his basic science is, or finds no use for it."

About the time Pruyser's book appeared, another

prominent figure, more closely identified with the pastoral care field, sounded a similar but more urgent alarm. If Pruyser feels we have lost religion, Don Browning of the University of Chicago (itself no hotbed of conservatism) claims we have lost morality—or more accurately, the "moral context of pastoral care."[2] Browning contends, in his book by that title, that modern pastoral care has become preoccupied with emotional dynamics and growth, and the resolution of intrapsychic and interpersonal conflict. Such matters, Browning feels, belong more properly to psychotherapy, from which indeed they were appropriated in the first place. Ministry, however, should have as its primary aim to "help shape the moral universe of values and meanings" by which life can be responsibly conducted. Browning therefore wishes to reassert the traditional Judeo-Christian emphasis on the moral and rational ordering of daily life. Today moral uncertainty and confusion are widespread, and can only be compounded if ministry continues to divert its attention from moral guidance to attempts at helping persons with emotional and psychotherapeutic problems. "At a time," he writes, "when moral clarification is most needed because normative cultural values are in a state of crisis, pastoral care and counseling have, for the most part, abandoned the task of moral guidance. . . . The tough value issues are [therefore] left up to the individual's tastes and preferences."

I suspect that, apart from the originality of their analyses and proposed solutions, Pruyser and Browning are voicing concerns that also lurk just beneath the clinically smooth surface of many modern pastors who wonder, in their day to day pastoral care, whatever became of religion and moral guidance in the ministry. Yet behind this concern lies a more serious problem: for some years pastoral care and systematic theology have maintained a polite but distant and not entirely respectful relationship with one another. Not only has pastoral care imbibed heavily from the enchanted springs of secular psychology, but theology for its part has often seemed far removed from the pain and perplexity of ordinary human problems. It is therefore not surprising to hear pastors and theologians alike lamenting the loss of theology in pastoral care.

The problem behind the questions raised by Pruyser and Browning is theological. Only when pastoral care recovers a sense of operating decisively and distinctively out of a theological perspective can these questions be adequately answered. Pruyser writes as a psychologist, Browning in essence as a religious philosopher, neither as a theologian; yet both books are struggling with an issue that, in my judgment, is theological in nature. The basic problem requiring attention has to do with what pastoral care should be, normatively; and this, in turn, is a question of how our caring as pastors participates in the saving work of God's Spirit in the world. The dilemma of contemporary pastoral care—its loss of distinctive identity and purpose—is foremost a theological problem.

While this problem could be explored from a number of perspectives, it may be especially helpful to think it through in dialogue with Jürgen Moltmann's theology, precisely because Moltmann seeks to articulate the distinctiveness of the biblical witness over against prevailing cultural beliefs and values. If pastoral ministry in America is bourgeois and culture-bound, Moltmann's radical emphasis on the cross and resurrection may offer a salutory corrective for rethinking pastoral care in an explicitly confessional, Christian frame of reference.

In what follows I shall attempt to elucidate what some of these correctives and new directions might be for pastoral theory. It will be my contention that Moltmann's theology, despite its own conceptual and methodological problems which I will not pursue here, can make a significant contribution toward solving pastoral care's identity crisis. This possibility stems partly from its power to expose unrecognized religious assumptions in our theory and practice, and partly from the vision of God and human life it proposes, which, if taken as a guiding vision for ministry, would inevitably reorient aspects of contemporary pastoral practice and endow it with a more distinctively Christian identity.[3]

To make this point, it will first be necessary to bring into focus certain major themes in Moltmann's thought, as well as certain cardinal principles of contemporary pastoral care. Thus in what follows we shall turn first to Moltmann's exposition of the meaning of the cross for Christian theology in *The Crucified God* and other works. Next we will consider what might be regarded as a typical instance of modern pastoral care according to the progressive clinical tradition in order to illustrate and identify the foundational values of contemporary practice. With theological and pastoral themes thus clarified, we may then be in a position to explore in concrete, practical detail, the potential contributions of Moltmann's theology for solving the dilemma of contemporary pastoral care.

I.

In *The Crucified God* Moltmann interprets Jesus as one who was completely identified with the coming of God's kingdom and hence with God, yet one given over to a fate of suffering and death as if he were a complete outcast, a stranger to God, numbered among thieves and transgressors, and abandoned to a lonely, Godforsaken death. Probing this contrast, Moltmann concludes that the cross implies some sort of distinction within the being of God itself, in that the One totally identified with God is also the One utterly abandoned by God—a conflict, as it were, "between God and God," or in traditional terms, between Father and Son.[4] Thus the cross impels theology toward fundamental distinctions within God, and ultimately, in Moltmann's exposition, toward trinitarianism. The God of Jesus cannot be monotheistic in the ordinary sense, and Christian theology cannot be a "radical monotheism" as H. Richard Niebuhr maintained. It must rather be trinitarian theology in which distinctions are perceived between the grieving Father and the abandoned, Godforsaken Son, as they are found together and fulfilled in mutual love through the power of the Spirit.

Moltmann therefore emphasizes God's radical openness to, involvement in, and identification with all that can be summed up in the term, "Godforsakenness." Jesus, the One completely identified with God in his proclamation of the coming Kingdom, is put to death like an ordinary blasphemer and criminal, and dies among the poor and despised, the losers and rejects of history. God therefore stands with them and indeed becomes one of them—outside the bounds of respectability and morality—poor, rejected, Godforsaken, dead. In this final act of identification the cross brings the profound inner movement of Jesus' ministry to its full and final conclusion, for he came preaching the good news of the Kingdom to the poor, the sinful, the rejected, the "lost sheep of the house of Israel," and not to the powerful, the rich, or the righteous. "Blessed are the poor in spirit, for theirs is the kingdom of heaven." On the cross Jesus was utterly one with them even as he was utterly one with God. Hence Moltmann can say that through Jesus God actually experiences Godforsakenness, sin, and death, saying not that God dies, but that death is "in God."[5]

By the same token, however, it is *God* for whom the powers of sin and death cannot prevail, who identifies with the Godless. By his identification with Godforsakenness, God raises his crucified Son to new life and with him, through the power of the Spirit, all the Godforsaken, sinful, poor, oppressed, and dying of the earth. It is the broken sinner, the hopelessly suffering, the cruelly oppressed, the dying and the dead—all who are the losers and the lost by the world's standards—who inherit the kingdom of God's love, together with all who identify with them in their need. To them belongs the future of God when even the dead shall be raised and the meek shall inherit the earth. The gospel, therefore, reverses everything we would ordinarily expect to be in the divine scheme of things concerning life, religion, and morality—and even God. For this crucified God loves the losers and suffers for them; and sinners, who truly deserve nothing, are forgiven and blessed.

A call to faith in such a gospel must be a call to trust and hope in the coming of the kingdom of this strangely crucified God. It must be the announcement of good news to the poor, and a call to mission, a call, so to speak, to throw in our lot, heart and soul, with the poor and oppressed, to care preeminently and passionately for those who live at the margins or on the underside of respectability, power, and righteousness, for all who are "poor"—whether economically, politically, socially, psychologically, or morally. Such a life, hidden with Christ in the crucified God, is freed from the anxious concerns of status, power, health, wealth, or righteousness. The Christian is called to live for and among the sinful and the suffering and thus as one already dead, yet alive in the Spirit, free, loving, and joyful, buoyed up and enlivened by hope in the very midst of suffering and hopelessness. Such hope far surpasses ordinary optimism which asserts itself against a still threatening future by an effort of positive thinking or emotional enthusiasm, however much wisely and cautiously tempered. Hope in the Spirit is a "hope against hope," a hope that lives beyond destruction in the power of God.[6] It is therefore hope in the future of the crucified God.

These themes, which form the central vision of Moltmann's thought, would seem to have obvious and immediate implications for pastoral care, if only because pastoral care is preeminently concerned with God's presence in suffering. For in pastoral experience, theological vision and human struggle meet face to face. It is therefore appropriate that we turn next to a report of an actual instance of such a ministry in the hope that, by pondering its pain and mystery, we may see more clearly how vision and care can come together, or what it might mean for them to do so. Specifically, we shall hope to see, in this instance of modern pastoral care, how Moltmann's vision of the crucified God can help us gain perspective on our current practice, and perhaps point the way to finding a more authentically Christian style of ministry for our time.

II.

The incident concerns a sixty-two-year-old black woman—a "Mrs. B."—with whom I became acquainted during her recovery from surgery in a hospital where I was chaplain. I do not propose that my ministry with her illustrates any state of pastoral perfection, but it does, I believe, offer a fairly representative sampling of the style and method of clinically informed pastoral care in America today. And, as I shall show, it also illustrates reasonably well what I regard as a virtual consensus today concerning the basic operating principles in pastoral work—the assumptions we make about "how to do it."

It was afternoon, and I found Mrs. B. in her wheelchair near the bed. She greeted me warmly. I noticed, with a slight chill, the stump of her leg, amputated just above the knee and heavily bandaged, protruding from beneath her housecoat. Soon, however, we were engaged in a friendly chat—something about a problem with her wheelchair—when another patient, a young black man, lying face down on a mobile stretcher, wheeled himself by the door and said hello to Mrs. B. He was a burn patient and had been in the hospital many weeks. When he had wheeled himself on down the hall, Mrs. B., somewhat wistfully, observed, "You know, you see a lot of things up here."

"Yes," I said, "you do."

"And some of 'em don't make it. We've lost a couple."

This sudden, oblique reference to death stirred my own anxieties. "Mmmmm," I said, "did you know them at all?"

"No, I didn't," she replied, "but you are sort of aware of it happening, you know . . ."

I wondered, half fearfully, what she was about to say next. When she did not continue, I said, "Yes, I am sure you are. I guess when you're in the hospital you sort of live with it more than normally, more aware of death than when you're on the outside."

"Yes," she replied, "I think so . . . I've been up here over seven weeks now—almost two months."

"Getting to seem like a pretty long time, I imagine."

"Oh yes, it does, an awfully long time . . . but the doctor says I'm getting better. I still don't know when I'll be going home, but I'm leaving that up to him. He says I'm getting better, and I'll just let him decide when."

With this, Mrs. B. seemed genuinely hopeful, and I was quickly moved to respond: "I'm glad to hear that with all of this you've been through you do have some good news. Must be good to hear that."

"Yes, it is," she said. "I've been going down to therapy in the basement and they're going to start me with the walker soon."

"So you're beginning to feel some progress now," I said. Our talk continued in this hopeful vein for a few minutes, but soon her tone deepened again. "They want to fit my leg fairly soon," she said with a deep sigh, "but I don't want them to rush it. I want to be really ready for it; the stump has to be well-healed, you know, or you can just go back and make more trouble for it . . . I want to make sure I'm ready . . . You wouldn't want to fit it before it's ready."

"No, I see what you mean," I said. "Sounds like you can see these hopeful things coming, but that you don't really feel that you can just jump into all of that yet; sort of like you're still coming through this whole thing."

"That's right," she sighed, "tha-a-a-at's right . . ."

"Kind of like walking, new legs, and so on, are still sort of down the road ahead of you," I said. "You're looking ahead, but don't really feel that you're there yet."

"Tha-a-a-t's right," she said. "I don't. Sometimes I guess I just get too discouraged"—more deep sighing—"but that's right, I'm not there yet."

"Uh-huh," I said quietly. "It's been a big loss for you."

"Yes, a loss. A loss. It's been a big loss, a real loss," she said very slowly, with deep, rhythmical breathing. "Just like in the morning when I wake up, I start to get out of bed, you know, and then remember that I can't unless I get help. I'm just not used to that, having to have people do things like that for me."

"It's been a big loss in *many* ways for you?" I asked.

"Yes," she replied, "so much has changed, you know. . . . So much has changed, I sometimes wonder if there's anything left to go on for, but then I'm still alive and there are some who don't make it, and there must be a reason for that, and I'm just thankful to be alive."

She said this slowly and with a certain weightiness. I replied, "Many things have changed, but perhaps some things do continue for you, too."

This was more or less the end of our conversation. And, for me at least, it *felt* concluded, as if we had had a deeply personal encounter in which the ebb and flow of her feelings had been touched, felt, shared, and allowed to be. Before I left, however, she mentioned, in a warm and hopeful tone, that she looked forward to attending services in the hospital chapel. I naturally welcomed and encouraged her to do so, and added a happy reminder of the time a few days before when she had sung a gospel hymn for me from her bed. It had been so rich and soulful, in such contrast to the bustle and efficiency of the hospital ward. She blushed with gratitude at my remark, apologized needlessly for her voice, and promised to sing again for me some day.

III.

Looking back on this pastoral encounter, it is not difficult to see in my own style of ministry, whatever its limitations, the enactment of certain *basic and widely accepted principles of modern pastoral care*. Indeed, these principles are so generally accepted and taken for granted as to constitute a virtual consensus in the profession. As we shall see, however, they carry with them certain theological assumptions which operate the more powerfully because they are unspoken, unquestioned, and largely unrecognized. What are these pastoral care principles as illustrated in this case?

First, this report shows the minister giving high priority to the task of listening openly, without prejudice or the intrusion of his own agenda, to what the parishioner was communicating and shaping his responses accordingly. Such listening involves getting beneath the manifest content of the words to the larger message intended. As the pastor in this instance, I tried to "hear" what Mrs. B. wished to say about death and dying, for example, despite her indirect approach to the subject and my own anxieties about it.

Second, contemporary pastoral care pays particular attention to the affective or emotional dimension of personal communication, which often provides a key for opening up processes of growth and healing. When Mrs. B. said, "And some of 'em don't make it," I responded to the felt anxiety that this expressed for her, rather than to the rational information she was imparting about the hospital census.

Third, pastoral care today finds special significance in negative feelings and points of felt conflict or ambivalence. I tried not to contradict Mrs. B.'s death-fear by diverting her attention to more pleasant subjects or dishing out superficial comfort, on the assumption, drawn from dynamic psychology, that personal growth and liberation are best achieved by working through such tensions rather than avoiding or suppressing them.

Fourth, we tend to view pastoral care today as a movement or process that emphasizes exploration, discovery, and growth of persons, rather than as an attempt to render specific acts of care or counsel in response to compartmentalized problems or needs. Hence our caring typically exhibits a flexible, flowing style of conversation with the somewhat indeterminate, open-ended quality of an ongoing "process."

To the principles of listening, feeling, the acceptance of negativity, and process, however, must be added a *fifth* and final principle that perhaps embraces and subsumes the others. This is the modern emphasis on personal relationship and existential involvement in pastoral care. Working pastorally with people, we believe, requires more than a warm heart; it draws upon a developed capacity to enter into and sustain personal relationships in which pastors are existentially exposed to the hurt, conflict, and suffering of their parishioners. Modern pastoral care and education have therefore increasingly emphasized the pastor's emotional maturity, self-knowledge, and capacity for interpersonal relationship as basic criteria for personal ministries.

Listening, feeling, openness to negativity, process, and relationship express some of the basic principles of contemporary pastoral care. However, as illustrated in this example, they may also point to its dilemma. One is immediately struck by the absence of specifically religious vocabulary or discussion with Mrs. B. This may be due to an idiosyncrasy of a particular visit or my own pastoral failing. More importantly, the absence of religious speech may not mean the absence of religious concern or perspective, either with Mrs. B. or myself. Nevertheless, one wonders how or in what sense this conversation is to be taken as a religious ministry other than by the fact that it was, sociologically speaking, performed by a person identified as a pastor. Perhaps, at one level, this is enough. But theologically we must press further. Was there any respect in which my being a Christian pastor distinctively shaped or influenced my ministry? Or should there have been?

IV.

If we view this pastoral conversation from the perspective of Moltmann's theology, we may be immediately impressed by the extent to which the pastoral involvement seems to express something of the spirit or direction of Moltmann's thought. Whatever my limitations, I did, evidently, succeed in getting involved openly with Mrs. B. in her suffering and doubt. Her somewhat oblique and off-handed references to death did not escape my attention, and my own anxieties did not substantially inhibit our conversation about it; rather, we seemed to talk intimately and openly with each other as best we could. In this Moltmann might readily see what he calls *sympatheia,* meaning an open willingness to become involved with and moved by the needs of another person, to care enough to be affected by the suffering of another and hence to suffer with and for them in some sense.[7] *Sympatheia* is therefore the opposite of what he calls *apathy,* or the resistance to passionate, open involvement with life, and corresponds to God's own *pathos,* or openness to the world. Out of such open involvement there flows, for God and for us, a movement or "history" of relationship. This is the history of Christ, the crucified God, with the world through the power of the Spirit. Here pastoral openness to the poor participates in the loving work of the crucified God.

Indeed, in this pastoral report, some manifestations of the Spirit are already visible. Though Mrs. B. is experiencing a time of painful uncertainty and transition, from a life she will never fully recover to one she cannot yet clearly envision, in her deep sighing and deepening entry into the fullness of her experience she begins, it seems to me, to find a new kind of freedom and hope. It is as if she is beginning to let go of her anxious hold on life, symbolized by the felt urgency of getting on with the healing process. In a partial but nonetheless real sense she is dying to herself and allowing her life to open up to a qualitatively new kind of love and hope. We see this expressed simply and beautifully in her closing comments about wanting to return to church, and in her promise that some day—perhaps not long now—she will sing for me again. Such emergent hope—tender, vital, and free—is the beginning of life in the power of the Spirit for Mrs. B.

But let us not stop at this point, for if we do we shall have once again fallen short of discovering what distinctive contribution theology can make to pastoral care. What we have seen so far is a theological confirmation, a sort of vote of confidence in the methods and principles of contemporary pastoral care—not a critique of the kind we must expect from a radical theology of the cross.

Of course, it may be that our pastoral principles and methods, that seem essentially secular to us, are in fact only thinly secularized versions of essentially Christian insights and values that have come back to us through the social and psychological sciences, unrecognized, like Joseph before his brothers in Egypt. Almost certainly there is some truth in this interpretation of contemporary psychology. Nevertheless, we must not too quickly assume that such a conclusion solves our theological problem, especially in view of the contrast between the strongly eschatological nature of Moltmann's theology and the seemingly comfortable spirit of natural process operating in this pastoral illustration. Where, in my ministry, is the eschatological tension between things as they are and things as they shall be? Where is the distinctive mark of Christian hope that is a hope *against* hope, a hope in the coming of an order of life that *reorients* us from ourselves to God and indeed ultimately changes us into his glorious likeness?

Viewed in this light, the case appears rather differently. Recall our closing exchange, "It's been a loss, a real loss," Mrs. B. said over and over, with sighs too deep for words. "So much has changed, you know. . . . Sometimes I wonder if there's anything left to go on for. But then I'm still alive and there are some who don't make it, and there must be a reason for that, and I'm just thankful to be alive. . . ."

"Many things have changed," I said, "but perhaps some things do continue for you, too." My intent in this last remark was to grasp in a single statement the ambiguity of her experience and thus let her know that I found its very contradictoriness acceptable and livable. I was also trying to tell her that all was not lost and that the process of reorganizing her life, though temporarily impeded, could eventually continue. It was thus what one might technically classify as a supportive or sustaining comment. But notice that it was built on the assumption that sustaining could best be accomplished by fundamentally honoring the ambiguity and emotional uncertainty of her experience, and trusting that her own life processes would eventually lead her forward.

There is something beautiful, of course, in this simple faith in the natural order, for that is what it basically is. While not denying the very important role that Mrs. B's own attitude must ultimately play in her recovery, I was assuming that a basic trust in the dialectical process of her feelings formed a necessary context for her own initiatives and might even enable or promote their fulfillment. In theological terms, I was honoring and trusting the essential goodness of creation.

But precisely at this point our theological suspicions may be aroused, if our theology, like Moltmann's, emphasizes eschatology as well as creation, and in fact gives eschatology a kind of comprehensive theological priority. In such a perspective, the temporal processes of life are seen in light of the End, the present in the light of God's future, and therefore the present reality of Mrs. B. in the perspective of who she is ultimately to become. For eschatological theology, the human problem is not to be who we are, but to begin being who we shall be, to be reoriented beyond our present reality toward the God who is to come, who makes all things new, who forgives the sinner and raises the dead.[8]

We have already noted that there was a kind of in-breaking of the kingdom—at least the beginning of an in-breaking—in the case of Mrs. B. What we are now in a position to see, however, is that my ministry was less one of eschatological hope against hope than a ministry of natural process, in which the ongoing feelings of hope and despair were simply accepted in their ambiguity and allowed to unfold. I rightly resisted the temptation to falsify this reality by imposing a one-sided, undialectical word of optimism, such as by assuring her that everything would be all right. But neither did I fully acknowledge the radical, unanswerable evil she had suffered, or invite her to place her trust and hope in the future of the crucified God. To use Moltmann's terms, the deadliness of death was not accepted, nor was the full liveliness of life in the Spirit enjoyed. Subtly, indirectly, quietly, I tried to deal with the inexplicable mystery of her suffering, her irreversible loss, her death-in-life, by absorbing its negativity into an inherently positive, naturalistic healing process, without remainder.

In this effort Mrs. B., we may note in passing, was partly involved herself. Her own good fortune in surviving the long hospital ordeal while others had died set her apart, she felt, from them, the dead and the dying. For this she was grateful; but in her gratitude she inwardly dissociated herself from them, and consequently protected herself in principle from their mortality. Indeed, she wondered if God had singled her out in some special way. The farthest thing from her mind, as from mine, was a God whose love claims nothing special for itself, but rather suffers death with the dead in order to bring to life those that are lost through the power of the Spirit.

It is a little ironic that theology, at this point, should turn the modern pastoral principle of openness against itself. It was precisely openness to experience that I thought I was enacting with Mrs. B., yet the effort to be open concealed a more subtle and hidden rejection of the crucified God. The trouble, surely, does not lie in the attempt to be open to Mrs. B.'s conflicting thoughts and feelings. The question is whether our openness functions in a context of openness to God—the crucified God who is coming to live and reign through the power of the Spirit. I "heard" Mrs. B., and in a significant sense she "heard" herself, but did either of us hear the gospel?

One could properly object, at this point, that this critique could perhaps apply to the empirical ministry I rendered in this particular instance, but not to the general principles of modern pastoral care that I have outlined. After all, it was precisely my attempt to follow those principles as closely as I could that seemed to open the door to the Spirit as far as it opened. We must not indict theory or tradition for an individual failing.

Yet, there is more involved here than a personal or pragmatic problem. Behind the difficulty in practice lies a difficulty in theory. For if pastoral *theory* is not rooted in eschatological faith, pastoral *practice* will inevitably function only as a process of the natural order, within the range of possibilities and hope given to that order.[9]

This is precisely the problem of contemporary pastoral care. Our very creed of openness to human experience either incorporates the divine into the human and the natural, making God the idolatrous extension of the human ego, in our own image, or abandons any concern about God whatsoever—or at least concern about God's "Godness," or otherness, over against our experience. Thus we have a ministry of the church falling victim to every fad and fancy of the psychoculture, from psychoanalysis to psychodrama, from TA to touchy-feely forms of encounter—all of which may offer something valuable to ministry—but none of which necessarily constitutes a ministry of faith. If pastoral care is to find its true identity, it must find its true God, the God of the cross and the resurrection, and conduct its ministry in the situation of the crucified God in the power of the Spirit.

V.

Rhetoric aside, however, you and I are practitioners as well as theologians and must therefore also try to think concretely about what these thoughts mean for, let us say, the specific care of Mrs. B. Putting the question crudely, what should I have said or done that I did not do? I say "crudely" because such a question already begs the theological point in a certain sense; our task is not a legalistic one of contriving acceptable words, but a matter of moral and spiritual discernment, and finally a matter of faith. However, unless we resort to a purely charismatic notion of pastoral care in which, like the New Testament apostles, it shall be given to us in that hour what to speak, we must at least begin to sketch the outlines of a pastoral methodology.

I confess that I myself, and probably all of us, are pioneers more than settlers on this question; the land seems strange and new. Allow me, therefore, in a spirit of exploration rather than certainty, to suggest two practical implications of the theology of the cross for contemporary pastoral care.

First, Moltmann's theology of the cross impels us to find ways of identifying and focusing an *invitation to faith*—faith in the crucified God alive in the power of the Spirit. I had offered Mrs. B. a quiet trust in the healing processes of nature by accepting the ambiguities of her felt experience. This was certainly better than offering glib or pious assurances; yet it failed to provide a ministry of Christian hope. It failed to communicate that whether Mrs. B. recovered her physical functions *or not*, whether her life regained its usual meanings and patterns *or not*, indeed, whether she lived *or died*, she was a worthy human being whom nothing could separate from the love of the crucified God. Mrs. B. did not need to know the dialectical, trinitarian complexities of the love, being, and history of God. But she did need to hear the good news that no power in life or death, however devastating, could separate her from the strength of this God's love, and hence be invited to trust that her worth and future as a human being would be established and secure even in the midst of Godforsakenness and death.

Communicating this word, as James Fowler suggests elsewhere in this volume, requires the language of parable, story, and metaphor. Only such imaginative language can point beyond the self-enclosed structures of thought and belief by which we ordinarily live to a new order or possibility where neither sin nor death nor any power in creation is held ultimately against us. One pastoral task with Mrs. B. is therefore to find creative ways of "imaging" this vision with her.

Of course such images will not be exclusively or even

primarily biblical in many situations. However, in view of
Mrs. B's religious heritage and experience, a biblical image
such as one from the Twenty-third Psalm could be uniquely
helpful:

> Yea, though I walk through the valley
> of the shadow of death,
> I shall not fear, for thou art with me.

Such an image could, of course, invite sentimentality or
pious illusion rather than faith. It doubtless would do so if
offered simply as a conclusion or solution to her experience,
instead of as an invitation to explore it more deeply, to walk,
in fact, more faithfully through her valley of deep darkness.
But if this image were offered in a spirit of exploration, in
which not only her own loss was acknowledged, but also the
reality and anguish of this loss for God was taken as a
presupposition for exploration, a new and unexpected
horizon of possibility might open up for Mrs. B. In this
expanded horizon in which Mrs. B. would be invited to live
with her suffering rather than evade or reject it, her
Godforsakenness could cease to be a source of destructive
preoccupation with self and become instead a reality within
the larger reality of God, disclosing a vision of her ultimate,
that is eschatological, dignity and futurity as a human being
in community with God. The pastoral task is to "image" such
a vision and invite such a faith.

Second, we need to consider more seriously the call to
mission in pastoral care. This may seem inappropriate for
Mrs. B., because it would seem that her need is clearly to
receive loving care rather than be charged with the mission
of giving it. Yet Moltmann's theology might turn this
assumption around. To the extent that Mrs. B. lets go of her
anxious preoccupation or bondage to health and recovery,
as she begins to do in this conversation, and thus joins the
company of the crucified God, she begins to find a new life
and freedom making possible a new quality of loving care
for others—whose first manifestation may be the promise to
sing for me again—but whose larger future can be oriented
to loving care for all who, like herself, have known
something of the valley of the shadow. Surely the vision of

such lay ministry is not entirely inappropriate to entertain, whatever its actual form; for ours is a tradition in which we are healed by wounds, made rich by poverty, and brought to life through suffering and death.

It is not for us to say what Mrs. B's mission or vocation in her new situation may be. Theologically, we may say that to conform with the history of the crucified God it must be one in which Mrs. B.'s own suffering and loss become the basis out of which she serves and identifies with others, joining them in their need, and opening for them the gracious possibility of human worth and future whatever their state. In any case the pastoral concern here is to help her find and focus her vocation in mission.

Although pastoral theory usually extends to a concern for recovery of function and reintegration into one's social and cultural environment, this suggestion goes further by considering Mrs. B. not simply as a consumer of pastoral and other services, but also—simultaneously—as one who has something valuable to give even in her poverty of spirit. We may therefore encourage her to find expression for that which she may be uniquely in a position to offer to those around her. Indeed, the pastoral thrust ought to be a call, a challenge to such mission, not on grounds of health, but on theological grounds, as a necessary expression of faith in the crucified God living with us in the power of the Spirit.

Nor are we ourselves, as pastors, uninvolved in this trinitarian history of God with the world. Perhaps Mrs. B. will remind us that it is precisely the poor and the needy who, in faith and hope, have most to give; and perhaps it is we, strong and rich in our professionalism, who need most to receive. In the beautiful vision of Mrs. B. singing again, in the joy of the coming of God, there is an enduring message for all who would be pastors: the gift of her singing requires the humility of our receiving and calls us, like herself, to accept the poverty of the gospel and to find *our* mission out of the poverty of our own spirits, opening us ever again to the joy and liberation of the sons and daughters of God.

Future Christians
and Church Education
James W. Fowler

The theologian's job is to help us think straight and act true in our efforts to be the church. The theologian lives between scripture, tradition, and the unfolding present. He or she must have the courage and faith to bank everything on the Word of God and on the history of its interpretation. He or she must exercise the imagination, sustained by prayer and spirituality, to release the power of the original events of God's self-disclosure. There must be artistic power, fueled by a spirit that is holy, to communicate the master-images of the Christian faith so that the eyes of our minds and souls are illumined to see God's work in the present, and our hearts are moved to *do* the truth.

Church education consciously or unconsciously reflects a church's *operative* sense of mission. Teachers, curriculum, and program are of course the major intentional foci of our educational efforts, but the larger medium is the message. Our *real* sense of mission comes to expression, for young people and adults alike, in the priorities that guide our allocation of lay and professional energies, in the procedures by which corporate decisions are made, in our attention (or inattention) to issues of justice and fairness in the larger community, and in our seriousness (or lack of it) about being aggressive pioneers of expanding colonies of the kingdom of God.

Church education needs the critical and constructive help of church theologians. We need them in our efforts to find creative methods of engaging persons in the processes of becoming Christian. We need them in our efforts to stimulate development in faith. We require trusted brothers and sisters who know the Script and the present era, and who therefore can risk formulating the Christian story's present meanings. Without lively theological reflection and guidance in the shaping of its mission, the church is vulnerable to two kinds of failures. It will either pursue the route of institutional idolatry in which we produce good churchwomen and men for whom the church is an end in itself; or it will become a conforming cheerleader for the class and social interests of its members.

In this era we have good reason to be grateful for the efforts of church theologian, Jürgen Moltmann. I want to consider the import for church education of some of Moltmann's bold efforts to guide us aright toward present and future faithfulness in our mission to the world as followers of Jesus Christ.

I. Futurity and the Kingdom of God

The title of this chapter is "Future Christians and Church Education." With reference to "Future Christians" I intend a double play on words. I refer not only to Christians of the *future,* that is, the shape of Christian discipleship in the coming era, but also to Christians *of* the future, that is, Christians who lean into life, who are nerved and kept alert by the ever-fresh horizon of the coming kingdom of God.

The recovery of eschatology as the primary context for understanding Jesus' teachings about the kingdom of God is a great contribution of the theologians of hope.[1] When we begin to get their message we find that they have interrupted our sense of time in a very fundamental way. In commonsense ways of thinking we take for granted that the *present* is the result of things that happened or didn't happen in the past. And the *future,* we assume, will result from and be shaped by things that happen—or don't happen—today. Cause intersects cause producing effects. The present came to us out of the past; the past and the present will give us the future.

But commonsense understandings of time have to retreat

before the eschatological theologians' rethinking of our experience of time. *Present and past, they tell us, come to us out of the future.* This audacious reversal of commonsense understandings derives from the temporal structure of biblical revelation. Yahweh's acts of self-disclosure narrated in the Hebrew Bible take the form of *promise.* God reveals himself in terms of a living *covenant* and *promise.*

"I establish my covenant with you, that never again shall all flesh be cut off by the waters of a flood . . . ." (Gen. 9:11)

"Go from your country and your kindred and your father's house to the land that I will show you. And I will make of you a great nation. . . ." (Gen. 12:1-2)

"I WILL BE WHAT I WILL BE. . . . Say this to the people of Israel, I WILL BE has sent me to you. . . . The Lord, the God of your fathers . . . has appeared to me, saying, I have observed you and what has been done to you in Egypt; and I promise that I will bring you up out of the affliction of Egypt. . . ." (Exod. 3:13-17 alternate reading)[2]

Covenant implies promise—a commitment of the sovereign God to be *for Israel* and to make of her a great nation equipped to play a redemptive role in God's history. God's covenanting acts of self-disclosure reveal God's *futurity.* In receiving the covenant, therefore, Abraham, Noah, Moses—and all who followed them and looked to them— became people whose identity and future derived from the futurity of the faithful, promising God. In biblical revelation the question shifts from "What have you been?" and "What are you *being?*" to "What are you *being-toward? What future shapes your present and liberates you from your past?*"

Jesus' mission and ministry centered in the announcing and enacting of the coming kingdom of God. Story and act, teaching and miracle, calling and sending—all find their source in Jesus' powerful taste and feel for the closeness of God's futurity. The kingdom of God, God's future for us, *is at hand.* We are within its reach; it is already breaking into the everydayness of life. *Repent*—turn loose of your obsessive hold on the structures of the present and of your enslavedness to the past—open yourselves to the futurity to which God calls you.

John the Baptist preceded Jesus in announcing the

Kingdom. For John it loomed as a frightening specter, to come as a crushing judgment on the unrighteousness and the unfaithfulness of God's people. John's call for repentance and baptism is a call to return to the letter and spirit of the law. Baptism, a ritual cleansing, if received in true repentance, would set one right before the imminent coming of the judge of heaven and earth.

Jesus' preaching, in contrast, beckoned people forward into the in-breaking grace of God's powerful future. The nearness and presence of the kingdom in Jesus constituted a threat and judgment to those persons and institutions which had become blocked to their futurity in the Kingdom. Structures of antifuturity in temple and civil government felt the shockwaves from Jesus' assault on their bases of power. Sin, then and now, is rooted in enmity toward God's future.[3] Obsessed with our own survival, security, and significance and informed by images of the future which say "we are perishing," we human beings set about building castles of defensiveness. In religious, political, or economic power, and social or academic privilege, we seek structures for living which promise to protect us against the threatening power of the future. Now, as then, Jesus' message comes as threat and liberation: "Turn loose of your obsessive hold on those false shelters against the future you fear. Open your hearts and hands to the true power of the future; be reconciled to the futurity *God* wills for you; embrace your brothers and sisters in celebration of your shared futurity in the Lord's kingdom."

Present and past come to us out of the future. In his remarkable book on imagination Ray L. Hart puts it this way: "We understand out of the past; we live out of the future."[4] The Christian memory re-members the decisive events in which God disclosed himself as futurity—as the one who will be—as the one from whom our futurity, and that of the world, keeps proceeding. From those promising memories we are directed to the future in hope and trust, we are called to faith that the Lord will keep on meeting us on the horizon of the present, continuing his work of creation, governance, redemption, and liberation.

This recovery of the eschatological thrust of biblical

revelation has enabled Moltmann and other theologians of the future imaginatively to reconstrue some of the fundamental ways by which the church orients itself in the world. In Jesus' proclamation of the imminently coming kingdom the messianic hope of Israel found both intensification and universalization.[5] The in-breaking futurity of God's kingdom is shown forth as the unifying power for *all* presents and pasts. In ways that transcend even the metaphor "kingdom of God" there came to expression in Jesus and in his death and resurrection the disclosure of the universality of God as the power of the future. The radical power of the kingdom of God, as manifested in Jesus' teaching and demonstrative actions, was seen through his resurrection as the disclosure of a far wider human futurity. God became visible as the Power giving unity to all pasts and all presents through their shared futurity in him.[6]

The church is the community called to witness to the kingdom of God as the futurity of all beings. This gives the church no special status or authoritative prerogative. Rather it places it under a powerful mandate and responsibility. Through its witness of service and proclamation the church is called to awaken humanity to an awareness of our universal, shared futurity. By resisting patterns of life and behavior which deny the futurity of persons or groups, the church is called to make tangible God's commitment to the futurity of his creation. By constructive and reconstructive efforts to humanize the patterns of common life, it is called to align itself with God's work of governance and redemption in a world groaning toward the coming kingdom. By its readiness to suffer, to throw itself against the structures and forces of anti-futurity, the church shows forth the love of the God who submitted himself in Jesus Christ to the destructive powers that deny humanity's future in God.[7]

But where is such a church? How do we who are dazzled by the prospect of futures other than God's future become captives of the kingdom? How do we, who are obsessed by frightening and forbidding images of the future come to a liberating trust in the true power of the future which Jesus made visible? How do we who understand out of the present and live out of the past awaken to the promise of sovereign, redemptive futurity?

II. Advent: An Interlude

Let me change key and tell a story.

It began unpromisingly. It was the Thursday before Christmas. We were having a staff-faculty Christmas party in the School of Theology. The Professor of Church History had just read *The Year the Grinch Stole Christmas* to the delight of all. The Professor of New Testament then shared with us a recently uncovered scroll, of dubious authenticity, which implored Santa Claus to favor particular members of faculty and staff with humorous gifts. We were singing "Silent Night"—in Korean and English—when he appeared at the door.

Black leather jacket, blue jeans, rusty-blond beard and hair, a stocky six-footer carrying a black briefcase. Thick glasses with tinted lenses magnified blue eyes. The eyes. They arrested my attention. Intense yet spacy, they moved over the room. There was a hint of ominousness in his presence. From his briefcase, however, I concluded that he was probably just one of our graduate students, surfacing from the stacks for Christmas and looking for a conference with his advisor. I put him out of mind.

But twenty minutes later I passed him, obviously confused, in the hall. "Looking for someone?" I asked. "Yes," he answered, fixing his eyes upon me. "I'm looking for someone with theological training to help me determine the authenticity of a document I have transcribed." I groaned inwardly. Another con man with a theological come-on. But seeing that he was making a nuisance of himself with passersby, and fearing a bit for the people working in the hall, I said "Let me see if I can help you."

The document turned out to be a one-page typed affair which said, in so many words, "I am in search of the ghost of a dead man. I have reason to believe he was The Messiah. I am his brother. What does that now make me? Can someone tell me if I am who I believe I am?"

As I read the "document" I was forming a plan. It was a

beautiful day. Not wanting to get trapped in the office in a long, wasteful conversation which might end with my having to expel him forcibly, I suggested that we take a walk and talk. "I am more interested in you than in your document," I said. My plan was to part company with him a mile or so away on the far side of the campus. "Now tell me about yourself."

In stentorian tones, but not without eloquence, he began, "I was born in the year of our Lord 1946. I say the 'year of our Lord' because that is how we reckon time according to the Christian calendar. I am given to understand that the Aztecs had a far more accurate calendar before ours, but I shall speak of the year of our Lord.

"I am the older brother of a dead man," he continued. "You cannot be any older than dead. My brother, David Christopher—do you get the significance of the name— died in the Tet offensive of 1969. David—Christopher. My brother, I have reason to believe, was the heir to the throne of David. And now, he is dead. And who does that make me? I am Mark Matthew, christened Luke, older brother of David—Christopher. I am in the Book, you see. So who am I?

"I was in a church here last night in Atlanta and they sang 'And the government shall be upon his shoulders . . .' And I said to myself, 'I do not wish to be an emperor. I have no special qualifications to be an emperor.' But I have read *The Meditations of Marcus Aurelius;* therefore I do know something about the management of an empire. And the others have made such a mess of it, why should I not take it on? If it must be so, then so be it."

I merely listened, wondering what combination of losses and griefs, of constitutional instability, drug abuse, and the possible viewing of the recent movie, *Oh God,* had equipped this articulate young man with such a fund of deeply confused eloquence.

But as he talked on something strange began to happen in me. For he began to speak of a vision of justice and right-relatedness between human beings and between humanity and nature. In spite of myself I began to feel his words resonating powerfully with my stored memories of the prophetic language of Isaiah, Jeremiah, and Amos. As he talked about our readiness to waste young lives for the preservation of economic and social arrangements that exploit persons and rape nature, I felt myself becoming defensive. Not defensive against a crazy man whose disorientation was an offense to my grasp on reality, but defensive as one who knows the truth when he hears it, and resists it because it points up the inconsistencies and compromises which keep his life comfortable. Writings of Dostoyevski, R. D. Laing, and others haunted my consciousness. *Who* is the crazy one here? The one whose grasp of God's will is so clear that he is outraged at the blindness and complacency of privileged persons? Or the one who sees all this, but protects himself from radically facing it because his livelihood, status, and comfort depend upon there being a gap between God's righteousness and the structures of human life?

When we had walked a long way I said to him, "You know, I think you are very close to the truth. I believe you have an unusual grasp on the truth of God's will for us. But I must tell you, I do not believe you *are* the truth. That is, I do not believe you *are* the messiah."

"I do not wish to coerce your belief," he replied. "There is an infinite space between each of us. We do not need to conflict and collide. But do you think that because I came on Northwest Orient rather than a magic carpet I cannot be the messiah? Do you believe that because I am flesh and blood, a man like you, ordinary, feeling pain and rejection, I could not be the messiah?"

"I intend this as no put-down," I replied. "You are *close* to the truth. But you are not the messiah. I am grateful that you *do not* try to coerce me so that I would have to reject you or defend myself against you."

After this exchange he relaxed a bit, evidently reassured by my frankness and my readiness to be open to him. He spoke of his life, his vision, his loneliness, his experiences of mysticism and violence. And as we parted he gave me a sheaf of poetic writings in which he had written at length, and in confusion about the things of which we had spoken.

As we shook hands I had a strange sense of having been

gifted for Christmas. I was relieved that my mission of "helping" my companion out of the school had worked. But that was not the gift. Rather he was a gift to my imagination—a gift not altogether pleasant or altogether comprehensible. I felt a fresh apprehension of how his contemporaries might have experienced the presence of Jesus. Thrilling, mind-opening, frightening, threatening. Jarring to the structures of every-day reality, liberating, empowering, confronting, amazingly simple yet deep. Even as I whistled with astonishment at his confusion, I marveled at the profound power of some of the insights my companion had uttered.

This story and the real experience it describes are meant to open the way for some attention to imagination. Narrative addresses and awakens us in different ways than does conceptual prose. Narrative evokes images—images which represent and carry both sentiment and information, images which fuse emotion and orientation.

III. Jesus, Imagination, and the Kingdom of God

In 1881 Horace Bushnell—the Hartford, Connecticut, Congregational pastor-theologian famed for his earlier treatise *On Christian Nurture*—published another book, *Building Eras in Religion*.[8] In that book there is a chapter called "Our Gospel, a Gift to the Imagination." The gospel is a gift to the imagination because in its telling of the story of the Jesus-event, in its telling the narratives of his teachings and actions, of his death and resurrection, it awakens our capacity to imagine the coming kingdom of God. It awakens our ability to taste and feel the powerful truth of God's futurity for us and all people. It gives us images and heart to compose a transcendent reality, an alternate future; it gives us a radically new present and past.

I am beginning to suspect that the eschatological thrust of Jesus' ministry was misunderstood by most of his hearers. It may have been heard more accurately and threateningly by those who became his opponents than by those who became his disciples. When Jesus spoke of the coming kingdom and of the in-breaking of the divine rule, so vivid and powerful were the feelings and images he awakened that the "little ones"—the childlike oppressed, the poor, and the afflicted—literalized his promises and looked to the horizon to see the kingdom coming, even as we scan the skies for the appearance of a forecasted storm. Feeling prized and valued in the contagious love of Jesus, stirred by the in-breaking power in his miracles and parables, they felt the excitement of the imminent messianic banquet and the hope of jubilee.

But the kingdom Jesus spoke of may not have been something to which he pointed like a storm on the horizon so much as the image people formed of what they and life could be if they radically opened themselves to the future contained in God's promise. Their experience of God's gracious love in Jesus decisively altered the valence on their existence. To the perishing it bespoke a love which had the power and will to open eternal life. But to the *apathic*—Moltmann's suggestive name for the full ones who congratulated themselves on their piety and God's favor—the preaching of Jesus also meant a transvaluation of values.[9] "But many that are first will be last, and the last first" (Mark 10:31). In them, his message of the coming Kingdom inspired images of threat and subversion.

The rejection of Jesus by Pharisees and Zealots, and his crucifixion as a subversive by the Romans, has been powerfully retold in Moltmann's *The Crucified God*.[10] What needs to be affirmed here is that in friend and eventual foe alike, Jesus addressed the imagination. He addressed the eye of the heart and the emotions of the mind in such a way as to kindle the vision of God's glorious righteousness. His words and acts reverberated the conscious and unconscious memories of God's past promises and faithfulness. The order of his words and deeds enabled his hearers to taste and to feel the coming of the Lord. "Truly, I say to you, unless you turn and become like children you will never enter the kingdom of heaven" (Matt. 18:3). "He who has ears to hear, let him hear" (Mark 4:9). Only those with the openness to imagine could get his message. Only those whose grasp on everyday life was open enough to suffer interruption could be apprehended by the beautiful and terrible closeness of the sovereign God. Where will we find the church taking its mission and marching orders from alignment with the kingdom of God? Only where there is today the modesty, the repentance, and the imagination to follow Jesus in the present unfolding of God's liberating and redemptive futurity.

I have been speaking of imagination in what I hope proves to be a provocative way. I have meant to suggest, by implication, that—whatever else it was—*the power of the coming kingdom of God,* announced in Jesus' preaching, was and *is a function of his hearers' imaginations.*

If imagination were merely the fanciful, playful, childish *evasion* of reality which most of us have been taught that it is, then this statement I just made might border on blasphemy. If imagination were really the *opposite* of reality or truth, which our culture's commercialization and trivialization of it suggest, then my statement would be dangerous. But imagination is a much stouter and more central human organ than we have been taught. *Imagination, I maintain, is the principal human organ for knowing and responding to disclosures of transcendent Truth.*[11]

If we are oversimple about it I think we can clarify this claim for imagination's importance by spelling out three movements in this operation. When imagination is awakened by a reverberating new event or appearance it records the self's total response to the event. In response to any event which has that character of newness which we would call revelatory, the *first* impact is like that of a *solvent.* The struggle for a decisively new image, which can honor and conserve the impact of the revelatory experience, involves first the dissolution, or the disintegration of previous images. Put another way, the first imaginative response to a revelatory event is a *making strange and distant* of that which had been familiar, powerful, and taken for granted. Revelation, in the response it awakens in imagination, dissolves the "given." It cracks open the inert reality of the every-day.

Jesus' teachings and actions constituted events whose impact on his contemporaries was to crack open and make strange and suspect the unexamined images by which people lived. Healing on the Sabbath; eating food plucked from the fields on the Sabbath; conversing as an equal with the Samaritan woman at the well; *not* fasting and not observing rites of ritual cleansing; eating with tax collectors and sinners; the list goes on and on. The cumulative impact of these revelatory events, for those who had eyes to see, was to dissolve long-sanctioned images of righteousness and to negate expectations about the messiah.

A *second* movement in the imaginative response to revelatory events is the composition of new images by which to understand God, the neighbor, and the self. Jesus' ministry and parabolic communication were full of narratives and dramatic actions which evoke new images.

"A certain father had two sons . . ."
"A man was traveling from Jerusalem down to Jericho . . ."
"The kingdom of God is like a seed growing silently . . ."
"Unless your righteousness exceed that of the Pharisees . . ."
"There were five wise and five foolish virgins . . ."
"The kingdom of God is at hand . . ."
"Blessed are you poor, for yours is the kingdom of God . . ."

"The Spirit of the Lord is upon me, because he has annointed me to preach good news to the poor. He has sent me to proclaim release to the captives and recovering of sight to the blind, to set at liberty those who are oppressed, to proclaim the acceptable year of the Lord."

For any who heard him and observed him there was a host of new image-evoking experiences. Jesus, we might say, flooded the fallow fields of his hearers' imaginations, now stripped of the inert imagery of the previous every-day. He provided them with potent new images of a revolutionary relationship between the one he dared to re-image as *Abba* and those who responded to his call.

There is a *third* movement in imagination's response to relevatory events. It is a movement in which bodies and souls, activated by new images, begin to march in accordance with a new comprehensive master-image of life and reality. Imagination's powerful work of synthesis, or unifying into one, seems to require *doing* the new truth, *acting* in accordance with the new world-image. Only when the risk is taken of committing one's life in response to a total new vision, can the imagination complete its work of *knowing*. How clearly Paul understood these dynamics when he wrote, "If any one is in Christ that person is a new creation; the old has passed away, behold, the new has come" (II Cor. 5:17-18). Under the impact of a revelatory event, imagination dissolves the old and responds with new images and actions which, in a new unity, provide a transformed total experience of the world and of response and initiative within it. In just such a dramatic transformation do people respond to the impact of the gospel. The gospel is truly a gift to the imagination. In it present and past are received with dramatic newness from the Power that breaks in with liberating love from the horizons of our common future.

IV. The Kingdom of God and Education
for Creative Discipleship

Now let us focus what we have been saying about futurity, the kingdom of God, and imagination, on the question of church education.

We make a very important, even fateful choice when we *name* this activity which I have referred to as church education, and when we stipulate the master-images that depict its goals. I can think of no more powerful and authentic way of indicating the intentionality proper to church education than to appropriate some of Moltmann's terminology from his chapters in this book. Church education is—or ought to be—*Education for creative discipleship in the context of the coming kingdom of God.*

From the first this way of imaging church education pushes aside some other organizing themes or goals that have consciously or unconsciously guided the church's educational efforts. Education for creative discipleship in the context of the coming kingdom of God cannot be translated, without serious loss, into "education for character development" or "education for values and citizenship" or "education for self-actualization." Nor can it be translated, without deformity, into "education for churchpersonship" (to coin a phrase). Neither do "intentional religious socialization" nor "education for faith development" contain the normativity and radicality which we intend.[12] Though each of the educational approaches just mentioned may have important contributions to make to our task, the breadth and depth and thrust of what Moltmann intends necessarily spill over and relativize the categories of these other strategies.

Education for creative discipleship in the context of the coming kingdom of God is both a *function* of a church whose mission is centered in the coming kingdom and a *means* to the clarification and intensification of that mission. Unless the church's corporate vision already looks to the horizon of the coming kingdom, church education's work will inevitably tend to fall into the service of more limited and self-serving commitments. On the other hand, unless church education, understood in the broadest sense, is stimulating, goading, and guiding the extension of vision to the horizon of the future kingdom, there will be little chance of the church's finding its authentic mission. For a church, *metanoia*—repentance and new beginnings—must be constant and ongoing. Through such a process of *ongoing revolution,* under the consistent impact of the gospel, shared images of the coming kingdom can arise and redirect our loyalties and energies. Church education as education for creative discipleship must play a decisive role in precipitating and sustaining this ongoing church *metanoia.*

Does education for creative discipleship in the context of the coming kingdom of God necessarily stand critically over against culture and society? Or are there times and ways in which it must guide Christians into the tasks of maintaining and re-forming the *saeculum* (world)? Christian education cannot, I believe, determine in advance to be either consistently opposed to secular society (H. Richard Niebuhr's "Christ Against Culture") or consistently aligned with it (Niebuhr's "Christ of Culture").[13] Rather, what Christian education, as we are proposing it, calls for is an alert leaning into life, receiving new life from God, and attempting to respond faithfully to the movements of the coming kingdom in the present. Such a stance requires a *committed flexibility,* born of and tested in an *honest corporateness* and centered in an *imaginative, shared discernment* of the church's calling in the present.

Openness to the in-breaking Kingdom will never allow the sacralizing of the economic, political, or ecclesiastical status quo. Christians are called to constant and ongoing self-critical submission to the kingdom's imperatives of love and justice. These are corporate, social-structural imperatives. Moltmann and Segundo are right when they urge that Christians must identify with the oppressed and the exploited if we would really hear faithfully the liberating imperatives of the kingdom of God. Response to the kingdom has its constructive moments as well as its critical ones. Faithfulness to the kingdom may require profound investments in building or rebuilding the structures that maintain and protect the common life just as it may, in other contexts, require determined resistance, resolute opposition, or even dead-serious efforts to overthrow those structures. What *is* certain is that taking the emergent kingdom as the organizing principle for the church's mission and its education will mean that we will live in ongoing tension and transformational engagement with the surrounding world.

V. Imagination and the Ongoing Metanoia of Development in Faith

In concluding this essay I want to sketch the outlines of two major implications for Christian education arising from the focus on education for creative discipleship.

First, Christian education as advocated here must take seriously the role of imagination in knowing and responding to the coming kingdom of God.

Christian educators are perennially concerned about the place and role of scripture and doctrine in Christian education. Under the influence of secular education we are often pressed to clarify the concepts we wish to teach and the skills or behavior we want to result from our instructional efforts. There is obvious value in trying to reach clarity in these matters. But it is easy to let those concerns draw us into two kinds of errors in our thinking about church education. In the first place we may be led to think of the brief times of formal instruction, accompanied by set curricula and sequentially planned experiences, as *the* principal context of Christian education. And secondly, we may slip into an understanding of the learning process which is both neater and more sterile than education for creative discipleship can afford to be.

In recent years John Westerhoff has led in the effective critique of tendencies to reduce church education to the schooling model. He has called attention to the powerful "hidden curriculum" constituted by the larger institutional expressions of the church's mission and self-understanding. And he has proposed creative approaches to making the "hidden curriculum" serve the ends of an intentional Christian religious socialization.[14]

Less attention has been given, however, to *how "the content"* of Christian scriptures and tradition informs the process of becoming a Christian. Educational approaches informed by an older liberal theology and by progressivist educational assumptions have tended to think of the content, symbols, and themes of Christian faith in a somewhat utilitarian way. These play a role in defining certain virtues, attitudes, and values which are seen as desirable. In this context, the teaching of doctrine or Scripture seeks to serve the goal of nurturing these desirable virtues. Precise formulations of doctrinal meanings and methods involving memorization and content mastery are taken to be less important than providing a supportive environment in which experiences that nurture "Christian virtues" are encouraged.[15]

Educational approaches informed by neo-orthodox theologies, on the other hand, have sought to ground Christian education in the Scriptures and in doctrinal tradition. As part of their concern for right belief, they have tended to place emphasis on the proper understanding, in conceptual terms, of Christian doctrine and symbols. In conjunction with these emphases they have stressed the importance of teaching some skills for inquiry into the foundations of faith. They have wanted to provide grounding in approaches to Bible study and have aspired to make competent lay-theologians of youth and adults.[16]

The approach we are proposing here does not deny or negate the principal values of either of these two major orientations. In one sense it wants to combine their strengths. But it does operate with different assumptions than either of them about the interplay of faith and experience, and about how scripture, doctrine, and liturgy are foundational to education for discipleship.[17]

Education for creative discipleship sees personal faith as a stance toward life—formed in community and informed by commitment to God in Christ—that is mediated by decisive master-images of the Christian faith. Images are prior to concepts. Concepts result from the questioning and explication of our images. As we have said earlier, the gospel is a gift to the imagination. Christian education as set forth here will avoid the utilitarian use of scripture, doctrine, and liturgy into which liberal approaches have often fallen. And it will avoid the tendency of neo-orthodox strategies to make conceptual understandings of scripture and doctrine its prime concern. Rather, it will attempt to honor the hunger of faith for exposure to scripture, tradition, and liturgy as *stimuli for faith's imagination.* It will trust the power of the image-evoking elements of biblical narrative and ritual drama, and the language of Christian proclamation when it is used with conviction and congruence. Christian education for discipleship will take seriously the cultivation of imagination as the "organ" of human knowing in faith. It will sponsor approaches to the Bible and to prayer which encourage the generation of images and allow for the expression of accompanying feelings and emotions.[18] *But it will be faithful in holding the images so generated accountable to the normativity of the master-images which underlie and find expression in the Scriptures and in doctrine.* (The notion of master-images comes from H. Richard Niebuhr and Ray Hart.) Let me underscore the point that imagination, if faithful, submits its apprehensions and constructions to the constraining and guiding norms of scripture, tradition, and reason. The various "hermeneutics of suspicion," generated out of Marxist and psychoanalytic sources, become indispensable tools in this effort to keep imagination faithful.[19] This approach to Christian education will not leave cultivation of the imagination only to the domain of spirituality and contemplative prayer.[20] It will also focus on society and seek ways to expand imagination's ability to take the perspectives of persons and groups whose needs, oppressions, and rights cry out for vindication. Learning from the liberating theologies, it will insist on acts of effective identification with and service to the disenfranchised and the oppressed, knowing that the gospel and the imperatives of the coming kingdom impel imagination in quite different and truer directions when received from those vantage points.[21] Christian education must seek to expand the imagination to inform moral responsibility.[22]

This brings us to our second and final broad implication arising from this consideration of education for creative discipleship: *Christian education must expect individual development in faith and discipleship as part of the ongoing metanoia of the church; at the same time it must honor the diversity of capacities for discipleship in congregations and encourage the contributions of persons at each stage.*

Part of the mixed legacy of the Barthian domination of twentieth century continental Protestant theology has been its overall neglect of "the natural" in theological anthropology.[23] It has been deeply concerned to speak of the objectivity of God's self-revelation in Christ and to explicate God's inner-trinitarian unity which it considers indispensable to understanding the incarnation, crucifixion, and resurrection. But continental Protestant theology in the wake of Barth has devoted little attention to the "capacity" of human beings to receive and respond to revelation. From the Barthian perspective such a notion is replete with dangerous echoes of Schleiermacher, Troeltsch, *Kultur-Christentum* and the idea of the religious *a priori*.

Church educators, however, cannot afford to neglect the question of what human beings bring, by way of readiness to respond, to the encounter with the record of revelatory events and to tradition. Education, in simplest terms, is an intentional effort to bring persons into helpful relationship to that which will stimulate and provide the "matter" with which learning and growth can occur. The educator, therefore, must have some grasp and control of the "subject matter." But he or she must also have some purchase on the quality and shape of the readiness and needs of growing persons.

Life-span research into what we have come to call "faith development" has begun to shed light on the quality and shape of imagination's capacity to respond to revelatory events at different developmental stages.[24] Risky as such generalizations must inevitably be, they help us see how complex the task of church education can be, and how much—precisely in our *best* efforts—we must count on the guiding wisdom of the Holy Spirit. I close with a brief suggestion as to what the different, predictable stages in faith look like. I intend it as a celebration of the inter-play of the generations in the common growth and ongoing *metanoia* of the community of faith. I intend, in concluding with this tip of the hat to the *natural,* to thank God for the wisdom in creation which planted in the hearts of human beings a hunger, a restlessness, and an active and powerful imagination. And this, even as I thank God for the grace manifest in human history in One who became flesh, lived, died, and then lived again in order that we might *imagine more truly* and *realize more righteously* our destined communion with the One in whom we live, and move, and have our being.

And so I celebrate

—Early Childhood and the birth of imagination.

—Childhood and the delight in narrative and drama.

—Adolescence with its quest for personal truth and its romance of vision and fidelity.

—Young Adulthood, its thirst for ideology and the courage of the single eye.

—Adulthood and its suffering vicarage for the world.

—The saintly universal, with its costly actualization of the coming kingdom of God.

Christian Hope and the Black Experience

Noel L. Erskine

When Jürgen Moltmann calls for an eschatological faith that does not flee the world but struggles to bring the world into conformity with the new future of God, black Christians know what he is talking about. Indeed, it would be difficult to find a better example of the combination of profound trust in the eschatological promises of God with concrete application to the political and economic realities of this world than in the life of many black churches in America. Perhaps this combination has something to do with their roots in African thinking which includes an unwillingness to adopt the rigid time distinctions between past, present, and future found in conventional western thinking.[1] Both past and future are drawn into the present in a way that makes it quite impossible to keep future reality from having a practical impact on the present. As a result, the projection of eschatological hopes into an indefinite future, so common in white piety, did not become predominant in the black church. When black people sang, "Swing Low, Sweet Chariot," they were expressing not only a profound religious experience, they were referring to escape northward to freedom. "When the black slaves sang, 'I looked over Jordan and what did I see, Coming for to carry me home,' they were looking over the Ohio River."[2]

This unwillingness to put asunder what God has joined together—the eschatological and the concrete historical—which characterizes the black spiritual ethos is what has uniquely equipped the black church to undergird the long march toward freedom and equality of black people in this country. The only institution that could give birth to and sustain the civil rights movement was the black church. Before black people went out on the streets to be beaten by cops and torn by dogs, they entered the door of the black church to pray. It was not an accident that during the civil rights movement in Mississippi thirteen black churches were burned. The black church had become not only the symbol of hope but the agent of liberation for black people. It was the awareness of the presence of the despised and rejected One in its midst which enabled the black church to become the inspirational source, the organizational drive, and the sustaining power for a movement which might often have faltered and failed but for the conviction that Almighty God himself was committed to the struggle and would reward those who "endure to the end."

Moltmann's theology has given careful and systematic treatment to the themes that emerge out of the struggle with oppression. The critique at the end of this chapter in no wise lessens my own appreciation of the way in which Moltmann, by candidly facing the forces which threaten Christian hope, has helped put the issue of oppression on the agenda of theology. Moreover, since the advent of Black Theology in North America and Liberation Theology in Latin America, the Christian church can no longer talk meaningfully about Christian hope without relating it to the struggle of oppressed people for liberation in history.

As the story of hope's vision for liberation unfolds, however, it must be kept in mind that the struggle for freedom is not only waged by a people whose skin color is black. The struggle includes all oppressed people whether men or women, all who are the victims of socio-economic and religious domination. Black hope, however, is an appropriate point of departure for our investigation of hope's relationship to liberation because in America black people best represent hope's struggle for freedom.

Hope is more than the anticipation of liberation. It is both the motive force and the shape of human liberation. When Paul points out in Colossians 1:27 that Christ is our hope, he links hope and the liberation of the oppressed. When oppressed people make the connection between hope and liberation they struggle to free themselves from bondage because "the Lord their God is in the midst of them" (Deut. 7:21). Hope then must become historical liberation, and this is certainly why in the New Testament hope is grounded historically in the incarnation of God, and why in order to understand hope in the black context we must first review the concrete history of the black experience.

Black History and the Hope for Liberation

Black people understood that although God was not limited to history, he was present in history as their savior, friend, and hope. The God who became their liberator was one who suffered with them at the hands of an unjust oppressor. This God was a helper in times of troubles. The prayer of a slave woman illustrates something of the connection black people made between hope and liberation:

Dear Massa Jesus, we all uns beg Ooner [you] come make us a call dis yere day. We is nutting but poor Etiopian women and people ain't tink much 'bout we. We ain't trust any of dem great high people for come to we Church, but do' you is de one great Massa, great too much dan massa Linkum, you ain't shame to care for we African people.

Come to me, dear Massa Jesus. De sun, he too hot too much, de road am dat long and boggy sandy and we ain't got no buggy for send and fetch Ooner [you]. But Massa, you member how you walked that hard walk up Calvary and ain't weary but tink about we all de way. We know you ain't weary for to come to we.[5]

Here Jesus is the oppressed One who in his identification with the oppressed brings them hope in their struggle. According to black people, Jesus as the oppressed One would "make de dumb to speak, de cripple walk, and give de blind his sight." Jesus could make a way where there was no way.

This hope in Jesus for liberation was not only from social deprivations and a cruel world but also from sin within. The hope of liberation was both for inner and outer transformation. And so the slaves would sing:

O Lord, I'm hungry
I want to be fed,
O Lord, I'm hungry
I want to be fed,
O feed me Jesus, feed me,
Feed me all my days.

O Lord, I'm naked
I want to be clothed,
O Lord, I'm naked
I want to be clothed,
O clothe me Jesus, clothe me,
Clothe me all my days.

O Lord, I'm sinful
I want to be saved,
O Lord, I'm sinful
I want to be saved,
O save me Jesus, save me,
Save me all my days.[4]

When appealing to the One who took on our flesh to liberate us, inner and outer, material and spiritual are conjoined.

How did white churches respond to the plight of black people? Most of them were so deeply enmeshed in the system that they were unable to pose a radical alternative to slavery as such. Instead their efforts were twofold, toward the amelioration of the worst aspects of slavery and the conversion of slaves to Christianity. A typical example of this is found in the actions of Bishop Fleetwood, the Bishop of London, who was the spiritual head of the Church of England in Virginia. In 1696 he intervened with the crown, with the result that royal instructions to Governor Culpepper included:

Ye shall endeavor to get a law passed for the restraining of any inhuman severity which by ill masters or overseers may be used towards their Christian servants or slaves. And you are also with the assistance of the Council and assembly, to find out the best means to facilitate and encourage the conversion of Negroes to the Christian religion.[5]

The English hierarchy as a whole was greatly concerned about the lack of success which the colonial church was having in converting black people in America to Christianity. In 1701, therefore, the Society for the Propagation of the Gospel in Foreign Parts was founded with the express purpose of christianizing the slaves. However the Society complained that many masters would not permit their slaves to be baptized or to attend classes for Christian instruction. As Bishop Fleetwood said in his annual address to the Society in 1710,

> I have reason to doubt, whether there be any exception of any people of ours, who cause their slaves to be baptised. What do these people think of Christ? . . . That he who came from heaven, to purchase to himself a Church with his own precious blood, should sit contented and behold with unconcern, those who profess themselves his servants, excluding from its gates those who would gladly enter if they might, and exercising no less cruelty to their souls (as far as they are able) than their bodies.[6]

In spite of the bishop's good intentions and his implicit questioning of the cruelties of the system, we can see in his words the fateful division which was to allow even the more humane elements in the white church to minister in good conscience to the souls of blacks while leaving their bodies in slavery.

Moreover, the contradictions in the system were soon evident in the Society itself when it found itself the owner of a plantation with slaves in the Caribbean. The eighteenth-century historian, Bryan Edwards, summarizes the dilemma:

> The Reverend Society established in Great Britain for propagating the gospel in foreign parts, are themselves under this very predicament. That Venerable Society hold a plantation in Barbados under a devise of Colonel Codrington; and they have found themselves not only under the disagreeable necessity of supporting the system of slavery which was bequeathed to them with the land, but are indeed also from the purest and best motives, to purchase a certain number of negroes annually, in order to divide the work and keep up the stock.[7]

After 1740, there was an opportunity for black people who lived on the frontier of Virginia to become a part of the great evangelical movement known as the Great Awakening. From 1740, and especially after 1760, large numbers of Methodist, Baptist, Presbyterian, and other preachers began preaching in the frontier counties of Virginia. Many of these preachers welcomed the slaves into the church, and black people in Virginia responded to the opportunity to attend church services. According to John Leland in his Virginia Chronicler:

> The poor slaves under all hardships, discover as great an inclination for Christian religion as the free born do. When they engage in the service of God, they spare no pains. It is nothing strange for them to walk twenty miles on Sunday morning to meeting, and back again at night. They are remarkable for learning a tune soon, and have melodious voices. . . . They seem in general to put more confidence in their own color, than they do in whites; when they attempt to preach, they seldom fail of being very zealous; their language is broken but they understand each other, and the whites may gain their ideas.[8]

The change that took place was that the church was able to convince many members of the plantocracy that the Christian slave was the best servant the planters could invest in. George Whitefield, who was certainly the most outstanding evangelist of the Great Awakening, remarked: "I challenge the whole world, to produce a single instance of the negro's being made a thorough Christian, and thereby a worse servant."[9] Whitefield was himself quite distraught at how black people were treated. "Your dogs," he said, "are caress'd and fondled at your tables; but your slaves, who are frequently styled Dogs and Beasts have not equal privilege. They are scarce permitted to pick up the crumbs which fall from their masters' tables."[10] Despite evangelist Whitefield's aversion to the treatment of black people, he owned eight Christian slaves by 1747; and after 1750 he purchased many more.

Another example of the meliorative approach which had the end effect of reinforcing slavery was Samuel Davis, the foremost Presbyterian preacher to Christian slaves during the eighteenth century. He claimed that more than a thousand slaves attended churches under his care.[11] Davis spoke of concern for their spiritual well-being, but demonstrated no interest in their liberation from human bondage. Davis did encourage the education of the slaves. He supplied them with religious books, and many were allowed to conduct their own religious services. He also published a little book, *The Duty of Christians,* which was addressed to slaveowners. Davis informed slaveowners that it was to their advantage to christianize the slaves because Christianity would make black people more faithful, honest, and diligent. "A good Christian is never a bad servant, for Christianity teaches obedience."[12] Some masters responded to the book by allowing their slaves to attend church services. But Davis did not make a connection between Christian hope and freedom in history for black people. The truth was that he

saw nothing in the institution of slavery that made it inconsistent with the Christian religion. Indeed, he pointed out that it was part of the order of Providence that some should be masters and others servants. Christianity did not destroy the relationship, but only regulated it.[13]

A contrasting position was taken by the Baptist General Committee in Virginia which in 1789 adopted a resolution that Christian slaves in Virginia should be set free. It read:

Resolved that slavery is a violent deprivation of the rights of nature, and inconsistent with a republican government; and we therefore recommend it to our brethren, to make use of every legal measure to extirpate this horrid evil from the land and pray almighty God that our honorable legislature may have it in their power to proclaim the great jubilee consistent with the principles of good policy.[14]

It must be noted, however, that the Baptist General Committee was not asking the church to participate in the liberation of the Christian slaves. The recommendation expressed was that "our honorable legislature may have it in their power to proclaim the great jubilee consistent with the principle of good policy." The Baptist General Committee had no power to impose its beliefs on the churches, so there may not have been any unanimity among the churches and associations.

What then was the impact of the Great Awakening on the Christian slaves in Virginia? We must conclude that there were still many masters in Virginia who were opposed to their slaves attending Christian worship. Indeed, "Many masters and overseers [would] well whip and torture the poor creature for going to meeting, even at night when work was done."[15] According to Herbert Klein, the evangelical churches, after a short period of Negro conversion and religious instruction, again conformed to planter opinion in the nineteenth century:

The Great Awakening in Colonial Virginia was the work of only a handful of ministers, and it never penetrated into the tidewater parishes where the overwhelming majority of slaves lived under Anglican masters. Even with the breakdown of the established Church in the 1780s and the tremendous growth of permanent Methodist, Baptist, and Presbyterian Church movements, the slaves in the plantation areas still found themselves under the domination of the Episcopalians. And by the 1840s, the great rendering of the evangelical churches into northern and southern branches assured the planters' domination of church attitudes toward the negro by all sects except the Quakers.[16]

What of the churches in the North? Did they make the connection between hope and liberation?

By coincidence, the year 1628 marked both the founding in New Amsterdam of the first congregation of the Dutch Reformed Church and the first importation of black slaves into the colony. Did this common history move the Dutch Reformed Church to make the connection between hope and liberation for black people? Professor Gerald Francis de Jong in his article, "The Dutch Reformed Church and Negro Slavery in Colonial America," points out that by the middle of the eighteenth century the Negro population in New York was about 15 percent and in New Jersey it was about 7½ percent. Black people in these colonies provided a ready-made labor force for the Dutch farmers who lived in the Hudson Valley and the Raritan and Minisink Valleys of New Jersey. Professor de Jong suggests that the members of the Dutch Reformed Church were among the greatest users of Negro slaves in New York and New Jersey.[17]

Even free black people living in the North were subject to indignities. In 1786 Richard Allen and Absalom Jones renounced their association with St. George's Methodist Church in Philadelphia, where Allen had been one of the preachers, after they were ordered to move as they knelt to pray in a section of the church reserved for white people. Their response was to gather other blacks in the congregation and walk out as a body. According to the renowned black historian, Lawrence Jones, the action of Richard Allen and his colleague should be seen as a protest against racism. Jones points out that both in the North and South, black people did not have "equal access to the ministerial services and resources of the church. Blacks were forced to occupy so-called 'Negro-pews' (which were often painted black), or they were assigned to pews in the gallery. Frequently they were not allowed to enter the churches at all, especially in the South, and had to listen to the services at open windows and doors." Jones informs us that it was not unusual for black people to be denied access to the Lord's table by white Christians. There were times when black people had to hold their own services in the basement of the church after white people had gone home.[18] Richard Allen ignited a flame of hope by leading black people to discover that the only context in which they were free to hope for liberation was the community which was despised and rejected by white folk; the black church became the only place where black people would hear—*you are somebody.*

While some whites quoted the Bible in order to maintain the status quo of slavery, there were others who found a message of liberation in the Scriptures and shared that message with slaves. Some white radicals taught the slaves to read the Bible. Others encouraged them to run away from their masters. The slaves were often aware of the stance adopted by Methodist and Quaker missionaries. "James Redpath of Malden, Massachusetts, who wrote a book on his travels through the South, said frankly that the slave holding class ought to be abolished and the overseers driven into the sea, 'as Christ once drove the swine; or chase them into the dismal swamps and black morasses of the South . . . . I would slay every man who attempted to resist the liberation of the slave.' "[19]

We have noted two approaches within the early church in America which illustrate its attitude toward Christian hope. On the one hand we have seen that the church did not make a connection between hope and liberation and hence could not offer historical liberation to the oppressed. On the other hand there were a few lonely voices crying in the wilderness of oppression that there was hope in history for the oppressed. Thus the white church in this country—with the exception of these lonely voices—proclaimed a version of hope which was intended to deny black people historical liberation in favor of release beyond the grave. We must now ask, what was the black response? Did black people accept this otherworldly hope and the postponement of liberation to the after-life?

As black people began to transpose white Christianity into an African key, a new theme emerged—hope as a symbol of protest. Black people began to see that they would have to take their destiny in their own hands if they ever expected to actualize the freedom the gospel promised them. And it was to the Good Book that they looked for the assurance of victory.

> You may talk about yo' King ob Gideon,
> You may talk about yo' man ob Saul,
> Dere's none like good ole Joshua,
> At de battle ob Jericho . . . .
>
> Up to de walls of Jericho,
> He marched with spear in han',
> "Go blow dem ram horns," Joshua cried,
> "Kasé de battle am in my hand."
>
> [After the horns and trumpets blow,]
> Joshua commanded de chillen to shout,
> An' de walls come tumblin' down.[20]

The white church interpreted the Bible in a way which sanctioned the status quo. Black people read the Bible in the light of a coming new order. Religion transported them into that new order about which they sang,

Git on board, little chillen
Git on board, little chillen
Git on board, little chillen
Dere's room for many a mo'.

De gospel train's a-coming
I hear it just at han',
I hear de wheels movin',
An rumblin' thro de lan'.

De fare is cheap, an' all can go,
De rich an' poor are dere,
No second class a-board dis train
No difference in de fare

Git on board, little chillen,
Git on board, little chillen,
Git on board, little chillen,
Dere's room for many a mo'.[21]

George Liele, one of the earliest black preachers in Georgia, was licensed to preach (c. 1775) after giving a trial sermon before a group of white ministers. Before escaping in 1783 with the British to Jamaica (where he founded the first Baptist Church in Kingston in 1784), Liele baptized Andrew Bryan who was to carry on his work in this country.[22] On January 20, 1788, Bryan became minister of the first African Baptist Church in Savannah. E. Franklin Frazier, in *The Negro Church in America,* suggests that both black and white people attended this Baptist meeting house, and therefore patrols were formed to observe the black church.[23] It was not long before Andrew Bryan was charged with using the gospel to foment insurrection. Bryan and fifty other slaves were tortured and flogged. White people slowly discovered that black people had made the connection between the gospel and human liberation. "When the lash was cutting the backs of . . .[people] like Bryan . . . [and his fellow slaves] the thought was burned into their flesh with every blow, that for all their protestations, the slave-holding Christians knew that their system was doomed because it was abhorrent to the God they professed to serve."[24]

The mighty wind of hope blew messages of liberation through other slave communities. As Denmark Vesey and others planned in 1822 to initiate violent change in Charleston, South Carolina, black Methodists prayed almost every night for divine leading. Nat Turner, a black preacher in Southampton County, Virginia, led his followers in a bloody revolution in 1831. The participants in both of these ill-fated revolts understood themselves to be acting out of divine inspiration and in accordance with the Scriptures.[25]

Though put down, the spirit which insisted on concrete political liberation as the fulfillment of Christian promises could not be defeated. Emancipation in 1863 only intensified the determination of black people never again to submit to slavery in any form. This conviction was to reemerge in the civil rights movement of the twentieth century, when Martin Luther King, Jr. became the classic representation of the same spirit. King combined the most intense eschatological hopes for future blessedness with moral witness and political action in the present. In his life and ministry King was a true son and prophet of the black church whose dream for the future was informed not by starry-eyed idealism, but by the conviction that God is faithful to his promises. In concrete terms this meant for King that one day his children, and the children of all black people, would be judged not by the color of their skin but by the content of their character.

Moltmann and the Black Experience

What does this recital of the history of the oppression of black people in this country have to do with our dialogue with Jürgen Moltmann?

On the one hand it enables us to see why Moltmann's theology has been greeted with enthusiasm by many black theologians. Here, finally, is a white theologian who understands the gospel in a way akin to the insights granted black Christians by virtue of their long history of suffering. Moreover, Moltmann has been quick to recognize the contributions of Black Theology. He has not only spoken out against racism, he has defended the right of black people and other oppressed peoples to pursue their goals with more aggressive means where non-violent efforts have proved to be of no avail.[26] The resulting dialogue has been fruitful for both positions.[27] It is not surprising therefore, that James Cone almost made a Black Theologian of Moltmann, so great was the congruency he saw in their positions. According to Cone, Moltmann reinforces the black insistence that God's promise means "that the church cannot accept the present reality of things as God's intention for humanity." To know God is to know "that the present is incongruous with the expected future." The result is a holy impatience with the world as it is.

It is not possible to know what the world can and ought to be and still be content with excuses for the destruction of human beings. . . . Why do we behave as if the present is a fixed reality not susceptible of radical change? As long as we look at the resurrection of Christ and the expected 'end,' we cannot reconcile ourselves to the things of the present that contradict his presence.[28]

Another exponent of Black Theology whose thought reveals the influence of Moltmann is Major Jones, the author of *Black Awareness: A Theology of Hope.* His was an early response in the application of the themes of the theology of hope to the situation of black people in America. Jones sees black awareness as grounded in a sense of positive self-worth under a God who calls upon black people to deliver themselves from bondage and their oppressors from folly. Only a powerful conviction about their identity, their mission, and their future can sustain black people in the face of inevitable opposition and discouragements.[29]

The congruencies and parallels between the concerns of Moltmann and Black Theology should not, on the other hand, blind us to crucial differences between the two. Nor should we assume that Moltmann's theology, taken over lock, stock, and barrel, is appropriate to the American scene. Precisely because he is a world theologian who strives to keep his categories universal, Moltmann may prevent us from seeing the theological necessities close at hand.

Latin American theologians were the first to point this out. They claim that Moltmann, in opting for the stance of "critical theory," tries to create for theology a neutral ground over and above all ideological camps.[30] According to this scheme of things, the theologian plays the role of the universal critic who, on the basis of the perfection of the kingdom of God, calls into question every concrete political movement and economic alternative. Such independence and unrelenting criticism is supposedly necessary out of loyalty to the absoluteness of the kingdom of God, lest theology be identified with—and therefore serve the purposes of—any single movement or ideology. (The shadow of the experience of the German Church with Nazism, which sought to co-opt German theology for its own purposes, undoubtedly lies behind Moltmann's unwillingness to commit theology to the role of handmaid for any political cause and his insistence on a consistently critical stance.) As Jose Miguez Bonino comments, however, far from being genuinely universal, this critical stance is in the pattern of the European Enlightenment and results in an idealism that floats above the real world of concrete political and economic options, an idealism that avoids a commitment to put its shoulder to the wheel of those specific alternatives that are most consistent with the gospel. "There is no divine politics or economics," says Miguez Bonino, "but this means that we must resolutely use the best *human* politics and economics at our disposal."[31] God does not dwell at a critical distance either above the world or in an indefinite future; he works in and through what is available in the world and calls upon us to meet him there.

From a black standpoint, a final difficulty inherent in a theology that locates God's being in the future is that it robs the present of the assurance of divine reality in our midst. From Moltmann's perspective, the distinction between present and future must be maintained in order that God's being (as future) not be compromised by identification with the present order. Only in this way can God be the radical alternative to this age. Black piety solves this problem, but not by appeal to what—in the black milieu—seem unnatural and rationalistic distinctions between present and future. The black church protects the sovereignty of God by its understanding of the Spirit. The Spirit is the presence of God experienced as a palpable reality. The Spirit cannot be defined, therefore, as Moltmann seems to suggest, simply as the living remembrance of the crucified and risen Christ coupled with a lively hope for the Kingdom.[32] Black people find it difficult to become enthusiastic about the "delayed gratification" that seems endemic to any Calvinistic position. It is the experience of God here and now that sustains them. Their confidence in the promises of future victory in God's kingdom is based on their experience of his sovereignty as overwhelming spiritual power now. They *know* he will win the battle. In this confidence they challenge the oppressive powers of this world.

Therefore, on the North American scene it is not enough to speak from a universal theological perspective and say that Jesus identifies with the oppressed, the *ochlos,* that great "mass without guidance and direction, the multitude without political and spiritual meaning, . . . who have no firm community, . . . who are unorganized and lack a collective identity."[33] This all sounds very good until one realizes that it can allow theology to remain in generalities. The pertinent fact that North American theologians must recognize, if we are not to give up the concreteness of the Incarnation in our own context, is that the disinherited peoples with whom Jesus identifies are not nameless, faceless, and countryless. Specifically, these people are *black,* their faces are *black,* their history is *black!* For American theologians to operate in ignorance of this fact, or indifference to it, while at the same time claiming to present universal Christian truth, would be in contradiction to the reality of the Incarnation. We must not be afraid to say that God takes on specificity in our own cultural situation as well as in the first century.

Does this mean that we lose all ability to criticize black people or black movements? By no means. But this criticism is grounded in solidarity with them and with their cause as the point at which God is at work in our particular corner of the globe making for justice and righteousness. Where he is, we must be.

Therefore, I conclude that Moltmann is of inestimable assistance in helping us to clarify the biblical underpinnings and theological principles that ought to inform our theologizing today. However, we would do well to go beyond his limitation of theology to the realm of universal critical principles to see and to grasp that for the sake of *all* people in this land God has made the black condition his own. It is here among us and specifically among black people that we can say most assuredly his Spirit is at work. The black church is the open door through which all who enter can learn what it is to hope and can discover for themselves how hope liberates.

Response
Jürgen Moltmann

"Theology, as a function of the Christian church, must serve the needs of the church." With this thesis Paul Tillich begins his *Systematic Theology*. Similar theses are to be found in the writings of the fathers of Dialectical Theology, Karl Barth, Emil Brunner, and Rudolf Bultmann. In the daily experience of congregations and pastors, however, is theology really a function of the church? Of what use is theology in practical life? Equally serious questions arise when the thesis is addressed to professional theologians today. Does the theology that we write and teach genuinely speak to the actual demands and needs of congregations and pastors? Do professional theologians in universities and seminaries really feel themselves to be in the first instance members of the community of Christ?

Often it seems as if theologians and local congregations are going separate ways. What theologians pursue is called academic theology. In congregations, by contrast, an anti-intellectual style of piety is disseminated. Theologians are regarded as dwelling in an ivory tower, while congregations are regarded as living in a theological backwater. A regretable situation indeed! This gap between theology and Christian life in the churches is reflected in theology itself in the growing gulf between systematic and practical theology. These disciplines are becoming more and more isolated from each other. While systematic theology concerns itself with process philosophy, Marxism, and linguistic analysis, practical theology takes over more and more the methods of psychology, sociology, and organization theory. As a result, what makes theology *Christian* theology—namely, the vision of God in Christ and concern for the Christian community in this world—is in danger of being lost in both disciplines.

It was for me personally a great experience to participate in the forty-third annual Ministers' Week at Emory University because the attempt was made by that convocation to place the actual mission of the church in the world at the heart of systematic and practical theology and to discover their points of mutuality. In the lectures and discussions we found that theology comes into its own when it responds to the needs of the church, and that the church rediscovers her certainty as the church of Christ when she takes theology seriously and makes use of it in her daily life. Considering the tendency in the western world to separate theology and church, such a meeting must be designated as highly significant. Many pastors and lay persons who participated will have felt this. For systematic and practical theologians the conference was an occasion to analyze their own disciplines critically. Do our academic work and research methods really serve Christ and his community, or have we in effect distanced ourselves from this goal? Fortunately all of the contributors siezed upon this question and took it with utmost seriousness, which resulted in a sense of personal community. But more important is the new community of effort in a common theological task that hopefully will result from these beginnings.

Rodney Hunter has presented the dilemma of contemporary *pastoral care* in an insightful and sympathetic way. Hunter's way of characterizing the state of the discipline— "I heard Mrs. B.; Mrs. B. heard me. But did we together hear the gospel?"—describes as accurately the German situation, both in the theory and practice of pastoral care, as it does the American. Something has fallen apart that in genuine Christian faith belongs in the deepest sense together: the gospel and life. There is of course a more doctrinaire and traditional form of pastoral care which could be typified as—"We listened together to the gospel. But I did not hear Mrs. B., and Mrs. B. did not hear me."

When hospital ministry follows this model the gospel becomes orthodox and sterile. The humanity of the person, his or her personal hopes and suffering, is largely ignored. Bible and prayer book in hand, the pastor goes from room to room, reads a few verses and prays, and quickly hurries on without regard to whether someone has heard or not. It is not surprising that in reaction to this insensitive kind of ministry an alternative approach has emerged which emphasizes sensitivity. It is also understandable when this results in less attention to the Bible and more to the life history of the patient. Nor is it surprising that the end result is less prayer and more encouragement of trust in the natural healing processes. As understandable as this "pastoral care from below" might be in opposition to the onesidedness of a "pastoral care from above," onesidedness is not overcome by its one-sided opposite, as Professor Hunter makes clear. One must think more comprehensively in order to integrate the truths of one-sided approaches. Eschatological hope comprises in fact both soul and body, both the individual and society, both heaven and earth. Eschatological hope says, "My flesh also shall rest in hope" (Ps. 16:9 KJV), because it hopes for a new, transformed body on a new earth. On the basis of this kind of hope I would like to reinforce a few of Hunter's observations.

1) Pastoral care is rooted in the call to the kingdom of God in which heaven and earth, and body and soul, will be made right. Pastoral care carries this mission into the life and suffering of individuals. In conversation it seeks not only to bring this announcement of the kingdom to expression, but to interpret the life of the individual as it now is in the context of the kingdom. To be sure, pastoral care interprets ordinary experiences, but it sees these experiences from an extraordinary perspective. One is enabled to recognize oneself and one's own suffering in the love and pain of God. If one understands oneself and one's suffering in this larger context, one is freed from isolation and lonely sorrow. Even a dying life is then meaningful because it will be taken up into God's kingdom. Pastoral care should bring together the new perspective of hope and non-directive reflection on life experiences. The

pastor should be neither a mere "sounding board" nor a dominating "preacher."

2) In hospital visitation the emphasis is not on argument but on life stories. It is an art to elicit, to hear, and to tell a life history. Everyone who tells a story interprets experiences, and in interpreting one finds the meaning of life. In much the same way one finds the Christian meaning of one's life when hearing or telling biblical stories, for the Christian meaning of one's life is discovered when the two stories flow together: the biblical story and the history of one's own life. In the science of hermeneutics this is called "the merging of horizons" (Gadamer). Because the Bible is a book of divine promises and human hopes it lends itself to being repeated and continued in personal life histories.

3) In pastoral care training today much value is placed upon the technique of non-directive conversation. This is as it should be. The perspective of faith and hope will become evident to the partner in such a conversation, however, only if the pastor not only speaks with him or her but also with God, i.e., only if he *prays*. This does not always mean a prayer with the patient. It does mean, however, a context of prayer in behalf of the patient before, during, and after a visit. This places the pastoral visit within the larger dialogue with God and relieves pastoral care to a certain extent from the loneliness by which it is often beset. It also corresponds to the true situation of theology. In Augustine's *Confessions* and in Anselm's theological writings prayer and exposition alternate with one another. Theology is after all done not just for human beings but for God.

4) Finally, I must confess that as a patient I had certain reservations about the expression "pastoral care." I felt myself somehow degraded by being the object of ministry and regarded as helpless and dependent. If pastoral care is a genuine conversation, it is between two persons, two subjects, who are on the way together. Who cares for whom is not yet determined. Would it not be better, instead of speaking of "pastoral care," to use again the old expression of the *mutua consolatio fratrum?* According to Luther, it is through "mutual caring of brothers and sisters" that the gospel is spread just as much as through preaching,

baptism, and the Lord's Supper. Where this mutual caring occurs nothing less than communion with Christ takes place. "For where two or three are gathered in my name, there am I in the midst of them." If pastoral care is mutual caring, it is the occasion for genuine community between persons. This is why pastoral care as mutual caring always transcends primal trust in the natural course of things.

If we look once more at the conversation that Professor Hunter reported, the dilemma of the pastor who visited the woman becomes obvious. Mrs. B. was at least as much his pastor as he was hers. In any case, if I sense the situation aright, he went from that encounter having been ministered to. And for that very reason he also came to have self-critical reservations about his methods. This is what a good pastor is, one who is prepared to be ministered to and who allows him or herself to be placed in question.

James W. Fowler has presented the dilemma of *Christian Education* in a similar way. He has taken his own approach and juxtaposed it with the basic ideas of the theology of hope. Out of this confrontation he has developed a new viewpoint, "education for creative discipleship in the context of the coming kingdom of God." Here also I wish less to criticize than to underscore a few thoughts.

1) The expression, "creative discipleship," sounds initially somewhat paradoxical. If persons become disciples they allow themselves to be determined by the one they follow. They imitate their leader, but they are not themselves creative. This impression is false, however. Discipleship *(Nachfolge)* is not imitation *(Nachahmung)*. Jesus did not call his disciples to imitate him but to participate in his messianic mission: "Preach as you go, saying, 'The kingdom of heaven is at hand.' Heal the sick, raise the dead, cleanse lepers, cast out demons" (Matt. 10:7f.). They are not called upon to help him carry his cross, but to take up their own cross (Matt. 10:38). The call to discipleship is therefore a call to responsible maturity in fellowship—yes, even friendship—with Jesus. Life in discipleship is life in messianic hope and means: (a) preparedness to be estranged from society ("the world"); (b) readiness to suffer for the sake of the kingdom of God; (c) openness to the imaginative creativity of a love

that seeks to liberate the world. As followers of Christ persons are at one and the same time prepared to suffer and to be creative. Both dimensions would have to be taken into consideration if the call to discipleship were to become the basic motif undergirding Christian education. Obedience to Christ leads us into suffering because we no longer regard the laws and orders of this world as holy and eternal. Discipleship to Christ frees us for creative imaginativeness because we seek first the kingdom of God and his righteousness. To give just one example: Discipleship commits us to non-violence. Therefore we must create peace!

2) Professor Fowler has ably shown how the hope that becomes concrete in repentance *(metanoia)* reverses all of life. This is the truth of the messianic proclamation of Jesus. The last shall be first! The poor are blessed!Sinners will be justified! The sick shall be healed! Wherever this messianic hope is proclaimed the normal course of life is interrupted; it is impossible to continue with business as usual. One turns from the past to the future—and is made free! By changing the direction of life new creative powers of the imagination are released and set free. As Fowler demonstrates, the expectation of the God who makes the impossible possible liberates our spirit from habitual routine and makes it creative. The categories of possibility, the new, freedom, and creative imagination belong together. They constitute life in repentance and hope.

I find it difficult, however, to combine these thoughts of repentance and hope with the basic notions of Christian education understood as faith development or religious socialization as Professor Fowler appears to wish to do. According to my understanding, development and growth belong to the realm of evolution and planning. In order to plan desirable developments in the sphere of human potentialities one doesn't really need creative fantasy but perhaps only a programmed computer. Planning for such developments presupposes certainty about what is to be desired. Modern sciences give us everything we wish; but unfortunately they do not tell us what we ought to wish for. It is just at this point however that the creative imagination enters. It investigates not the predictable future but the promised future, and therefore that which is worth desiring. The creative imagination places in question the taken-for-granted values and desires that unconsciously control us. Before Christian education enters upon the planning of faith development, it ought to immerse itself deeply in the pain and the joy of the reversal of our personal and social values. Every alert younger generation places in question not only the educational methods of the older generation but even more their deepest and most pervasive values in order to gain freedom for its own life and values. Education for repentance is no education for perpetuation of the past but training for personal discovery of the future. *Metanoia* goes deeper, therefore, than growth and development.

3) The conversion of life, or the reversal of the direction of life and its values, always begins with a great *wonder*. It is in bottomless amazement that we perceive the new and different future that the gospel proclaims. In endless wonder we forget the bonds of the past and open ourselves to the new future. Because the gospel produces this kind of astonishment in us it is a gift to our imagination. Should Christian education not begin with the experience of great astonishment regarding the wonder of the gospel?

Finally, **Noel L. Erskine** has set forth the striking and fruitful similarities between the theology of hope and *Black Theology*. Eschatological hope and the historical liberation of the oppressed belong together. Eschatological hope becomes concrete in historical liberation. At the same time, only through the battle for historical liberation does one learn the supportive power of eschatological hope. When this hope is reduced to otherworldliness, individualism, or to a limited redemption, it is falsified. At this point I would like to lift up what theologians of hope and black theologians have learned from their experiences and the direction in which their future tasks may therefore lie.

The basic concepts of the theology of hope came to me during the experiences of a three-year imprisonment as a POW after the Second World War. The experiences of imprisonment, humiliation, and exploitation, as well as the

yearning for, and dreams of, freedom on the other side of
the barbed wire, were the beginning. These basic ideas were
then developed during the decade of West German
rebuilding (1948-58). The commitment to social and political transformation and the dreams of a peaceful, democratic, and socially just world were the extension of that
original vision. Anyone whose mind and heart have been
stamped by such experiences can sympathize with the
victims of oppression. He or she knows their suffering and
shares their hope for freedom. Only out of our own
experience do we gain understanding of others. This has
nothing to do with "universalism," generalities, or abstrac-
tions; it is nothing less than *solidarity*.

Because the experiences of the imprisoned have similarities with the experiences of black slaves, it is not surprising
that there are congruencies between the theology of hope
and Black Theology just as there are between the theology
of hope and liberation theologies. Because the black
experience is so similar to the experience of the poor as "the
condemned of this world," there is also a convergence with
theologies emerging from the Third World. In imprisonment one learns solidarity with all who suffer degradation.
In much the same way a black person in the USA learns
solidarity with all of the oppressed. "Black" is a reality and
symbol of suffering in the same way that "imprisonment" is
a reality and symbol of degradation. If we understand that,
then it is high time to put to use the experiences and the
theological concepts that have emerged in the fight against a
slave-holding society, as well as the experiences and
theological concepts from the fight against fascist dictator-
ship, in the fight today against the oppression of peoples by
the northern industrial nations. Eschatological hope becomes concrete today in the actual freeing of the poor and
oppressed of the Third World. Because this is a battle for a
new and just world economic order, it will be fought out in
the First and Second Worlds as well. "Exploitation" and the
destructive power of "dominant" nations will be overcome
through the living power of "community" and "solidarity"—or the end is near! It is therefore necessary that the
various theologies of liberation, be they black, socialist,

feminist, or ecological, finally join together in a cooperative endeavor.

I add simply a brief personal word in response to Professor Erskine's critique. I frankly do not know who has designated me "a *world theologian*" (who is therefore obligated to keep his categories universal). I certainly have not raised myself to that status. Because, unlike many of the Latin American theologians of liberation, I am not Roman Catholic, I believe neither in the existence nor the necessity of a *theologia universalis*. As a Protestant I would criticize the notion of a universal and infallible doctrinal authority as a premature preempting of the kingdom of God by a triumphalist church. From the Catholic theologians of liberation we have as yet heard little criticism of the dogma of infallibility. How can a church which does not itself exhibit freedom free peoples? An authoritarian church has always promoted an authoritarian state, never democracy.

This book of lectures from the Atlanta conference has convinced me that a transatlantic dialogue is not only possible but exceedingly gratifying and unusually fruitful. For this I thank above all my friend Professor Runyon who originally conceived the idea that has come to fruition in this dialogue.

The Contributors

Jürgen Moltmann is professor of systematic theology at the University of Tübingen in Germany. His fascination with the phenomenon of human hope began when he was a young prisoner of war in a British POW camp, where he saw hope spell the difference between life and death. He returned to Germany in 1948 to study theology at Göttingen. After a period as a pastor in Bremen, he completed his doctorate at Göttingen and began his teaching career. He was called to the Church Seminary in Wuppertal and then to the University of Bonn. Since 1967, he has been at Tübingen. He has served on major committees of the World Council of Churches and the World Alliance of Reformed Churches. Among his works translated into English are *Theology of Hope; The Crucified God; The Church in the Power of the Spirit; Religion, Revolution and the Future; The Future of Hope; Hope and Planning; The Theology of Play; The Experiment Hope; The Gospel of Liberation* (sermons); and *The Passion for Life.*

M. Douglas Meeks is professor of theology and ethics at Eden Theological Seminary. A graduate of Southwestern in Memphis, he received his seminary and graduate training at Duke University. He studied with Professor Moltmann, first at Duke, when the latter was visiting professor there, and then at Tübingen. His book, *Origins of the Theology of Hope,* identifies him as a foremost interpreter of Moltmann in this country. He has translated Moltmann's *Religion, Revolution and the Future; The Experiment Hope;* and *The Passion for Life.*

Rodney J. Hunter is associate professor of pastoral theology at the Candler School of Theology. Educated at Yale (BA) and Princeton Theological Seminary (BD and PhD), he has worked closely with Seward Hiltner and has done extensive research on the phenomenon of commitment. He served as the chaplain in a youth correctional center in New Jersey before joining the Candler faculty in 1971. He is book review editor for *Pastoral Psychology* and an associate staff counselor, Georgia Association for Pastoral Care.

James W. Fowler is associate professor of theology and human development at Candler. Educated at Duke (BA), Drew (BD), and Harvard (PhD), he served as associate director with Carlyle Marney of the continuing education center for clergy, Interpreter's House, at Lake Junaluska, North Carolina. He returned to Harvard to teach in the Divinity School and to do post-doctoral work with Lawrence Kohlberg, applying the latter's theories of moral development to the process of growth in religious faith in an ongoing research project supported by the Joseph P. Kennedy, Jr. Foundation. He also taught Religious Education in Boston College's Department of Theology. He is author of *To See the Kingdom: The Theological Vision of H. Richard Niebuhr* and coauthor of *Life Maps: Conversations on the Journey of Faith.*

Noel L. Erskine is assistant professor of theology and ethics at Candler. A native of Jamaica, he has served churches in Jamaica and New York City. He received his first degree in theology from the University of London, a MTh from Duke, and his STM and PhD (under James Cone) from Union Theological Seminary in New York. He taught at Moravian Theological Seminary before joining the Candler faculty and is the author of *Black People and the Reformed Church in America.*

Theodore Runyon is professor of systematic theology at Candler. Educated at Lawrence (BA), Drew (BD); and Göttingen (DrTheol) universities, he has had pastoral experience in churches in Wisconsin, Brooklyn, and Philadelphia. He co-authored *Protestant Parish* and is editor of a volume that emerged from a previous Emory Minister's Week, *What the Spirit Is Saying to the Churches.* He has done post-doctoral work at the Universities of Göttingen, Constance, and Tübingen and is translator of Professor Moltmann's chapters for the present volume.

Notes

Introduction—Theodore Runyon

1. Jürgen Moltmann, *Theology of Hope* (New York: Harper, 1967).
2. Moltmann, *The Crucified God* (New York: Harper, 1974).
3. Moltmann, *The Church in the Power of the Spirit* (New York: Harper, 1977).
4. *Theology of Hope*, p. 243.
5. *Ibid.*, p. 25.
6. *Ibid.*, p. 325.
7. Moltmann, *Hope and Planning* (New York: Harper, 1971), p. 173.
8. Moltmann, *Religion, Revolution and the Future* (New York: Scribner's, 1969).
9. Moltmann, *The Experiment Hope,* ed. and trans., M. Douglas Meeks (Philadelphia: Fortress, 1975).
10. *Church in the Power of the Spirit,* p. 197 ff.
11. Dietrich Bonhoeffer, *Letters and Papers from Prison* (New York: Macmillan, 1953), Letters of July 16 and 18, 1944; pp. 220, 222.

The Diaconal Church in the Context of the Kingdom of God—*Jürgen Moltmann*

1. Rudolf Weth, "Diakonie am Wendepunkt," *Evangelische Theologie,* 36 (1976), 263 ff.

The Life Signs of the Spirit in the Fellowship Community of Christ—*Jürgen Moltmann*

1. Karl Barth, *Church Dogmatics,* Vol. IV, Part 2 (Edinburgh: T. & T. Clark, 1958), p. 55.
2. Cf. *"mysterion"* by G. Bornkamm in Kittel's *Theological Dictionary of the New Testament,* Vol. 4 (Grand Rapids: Eerdmans, 1965), pp. 802–28.

Moltmann's Contribution to Practical Theology—*M. Douglas Meeks*

1. H. Richard Niebuhr, *The Purpose of the Church and Its Ministry* (New York: Harper, 1956), p. 50. See also John T. McNeill, *A History of the Cure of Souls* (New York: Harper, 1951), pp. 108 ff.

2. Moltmann, *Crucified God*, pp. 235–78; *Church in the Power of the Spirit*, pp. 50–65; "Die trinitarische Geschichte Gottes," *Zukunft der Schöpfung* (Munich: Chr. Kaiser, 1977), pp. 89–104.
3. Moltmann, *Church in the Power of the Spirit*, pp. 294–314.
4. Howard Grimes, "What Is Practical Theology?" *Perkins Journal*, 30 (Spring 1977), 31. Cf. the first ten essays in *The New Shape of Pastoral Theology: Essays in Honor of Seward Hiltner*, ed., William B. Oglesby, Jr. (Nashville: Abingdon, 1969); A. V. Campbell, "Is Practical Theology Possible?" *Scottish Journal of Theology*, 25 (May 1972), 217–27.
5. Eduard Thurneysen, *A Theology of Pastoral Care* (Richmond: John Knox, 1962).
6. Barth, *Church Dogmatics*, Vol. I, Part 1, pp. 1–17 and passim.
7. See the essays in *New Shape of Pastoral Theology*.
8. Grimes, "What Is Practical Theology?" p. 32.
9. Cf. similarities with this method in John B. Cobb, Jr., *Theology and Pastoral Care* (Philadelphia: Fortress, 1977).
10. Friedrich Schleiermacher, *Brief Outline on the Study of Theology*, trans., Terrence N. Tice (Richmond: John Knox, 1966), pp. 91ff.; Barth, *Church Dogmatics*, pp. 4ff.
11. Moltmann, *Theology of Hope*, chaps. 1–3. See also M. Douglas Meeks, *Origins of the Theology of Hope* (Philadelphia: Fortress 1974), pp. 54–89.
12. Moltmann, *Theology of Hope*, pp. 197 ff., 325–38.
13. *Ibid.*, pp. 304–38.
14. Criticism of the uncritical use of psychotherapeutic theories in pastoral counseling is emerging from within the clinical pastoral movement itself. See, for example, Don Browning, *The Moral Context of Pastoral Care* (Philadelphia: Westminster, 1976); Paul Pruyser, *The Minister as Diagnostician, ibid;* Gaylord B. Noyce, "Has Ministry's Nerve Been Cut by the Pastoral Counseling Movement?" *The Christian Century* 95 (February, 1–8, 1978), pp. 103–14.
15. Moltmann, *Church in the Power of the Spirit*, pp. 295–314. See also Jürgen Moltmann, *The Passion for Life: A Messianic Lifestyle*, trans. with an Introduction by M. Douglas Meeks (Philadelphia: Fortress, 1978).

Moltmann's Theology of the Cross and the Dilemma of Contemporary Pastoral Care—*Rodney J. Hunter*

1. Pruyser, *Minister as Diagnostician*, pp. 27–28.
2. Browning, *Moral Context of Pastoral Care*, p. 25.
3. For practical reasons this lecture does not take up the reciprocal and perhaps equally important question of how this case material might provide critical response to Moltmann's theology.
4. Moltmann, *Crucified God*, pp. 151–52, 192–93.
5. *Ibid.*, pp. 207, 277–78.
6. Moltmann, *Experiment Hope*, pp. 36–37.
7. Moltmann, *Crucified God*, pp. 267-74.
8. Cf. Shirley C. Guthrie's helpful interpretation of Moltmann in "The Narcissism of American Piety: The Disease and the Cure," *The Journal of Pastoral Care*, 31 (December 1977), 220–29.
9. The "natural order" is assumed to include human society and personality insofar as their functioning may be understood as lawful phenomena within the larger sphere of nature, as generally assumed in the social sciences. Whether this conception of nature is philosophically or theologically adequate is open to question because it systematically

screens out questions of freedom and spirit. If such a view of nature is presupposed by pastoral theology, the issue becomes one of determining how such a conception of natural process would be modified by eschatological interpretations of creation and its transformation derived, as in Moltmann, from biblical categories.

Future Christians and Church Education—*James W. Fowler*

1. In addition to Moltmann's *Theology of Hope, Experiment Hope,* and *Church in the Power of the Spirit,* I have drawn on Pannenberg's seminal *Theology and the Kingdom of God* (Philadelphia: Westminster, 1969) and Peter Hodgson's *New Birth of Freedom* (Philadelphia: Fortress, 1976).
2. John Gray, in "The Book of Exodus," *Interpreter's One Volume Commentary on the Bible* (Nashville: Abingdon, 1971), p. 39, states that "I will be" is the preferred translation. Other commentators say it is permissible but not preferred. See Brevard Childs, *The Book of Exodus* (Philadelphia: Westminster, 1974), pp. 71, 75–76 and especially, Moltmann, *Theology of Hope,* ch. 2.
3. Pannenberg, *Theology and the Kingdom of God,* p. 69.
4. Ray L. Hart, *Unfinished Man and the Imagination* (New York: Herder & Herder, 1968), p. 307. See also Pannenberg, p. 72 ff.
5. Moltmann, *Theology of Hope,* pp. 141 ff.
6. Pannenberg, *Theology and the Kingdom of God,* pp. 72 ff.
7. See Moltmann, *Theology of Hope,* ch. 5 and *Church in the Power of the Spirit,* ch. 4.
8. Horace Bushnell, *Building Eras in Religion* (New York: Scribner's, 1881), pp. 249–85.
9. See Moltmann, *Experiment Hope,* pp. 69 ff. and *Church in the Power of the Spirit,* pp. 78 ff.
10. Especially ch. 4.
11. In this and the following passages I am deeply indebted to Hart's seminal work already cited. In addition I acknowledge with appreciation the ongoing importance for my approach to these matters of H. Richard Niebuhr's *The Meaning of Revelation* (New York: Macmillan, 1941) and William F. Lynch's *Images of Faith* (University of Notre Dame Press, 1973).
12. In referring to "intentional religious socialization" I have in mind the earlier work of John H. Westerhoff found in *Values for Tomorrow's Children* (Philadelphia: Pilgrim, 1970) and (with Gwen K. Neville) *Generation to Generation* (Philadelphia: Pilgrim 1974). My own research and theory of faith development constitute the target suggested by the phrase "education for faith development." See Fowler, "Toward a Developmental Perspective on Faith," in *Religious Education,* 69 (March–April 1974), pp. 207–19; "Stages in Faith: The Structural Developmental Approach" in *Values and Moral Education,* Thomas Hennessey, ed. (Paramus, N.J.: Paulist/Newman, 1976), pp. 173–211; "Faith Development Theory and the Aims of Religious Socialization" in *Emerging Issues in Religious Education,* G. Durka and J. Smith, eds., (Paramus, N.J.: Paulist/Newman, 1976), pp. 187–211; and Fowler, Keen, & Berryman, *Life Maps: Conversations on the Journey of Faith* (Waco, Texas: Word Books, 1978). Westerhoff draws on faith development materials in his widely influential book *Will Our Children Have Faith?* (New York: Seabury, 1976).

13. The references are to *Christ and Culture* (New York: Harper, 1951).

14. See Westerhoff's *Will Our Children* and *Generation to Generation.*

15. The position developed powerfully by George Albert Coe in the early decades of this century represents the prime fountainhead of this tendency. See *Educating for Citizenship* (New York: Scribner's, 1932); *Virtue and the Virtues,* reprint from Journal, National Education Association of the United States, 1911, pp. 419–25; and *Education in Religion and Morals* (Old Tappan, N.J.: F. H. Revell, 1904).

16. H. Shelton Smith's *Faith and Nurture* (New York: Scribner's, 1948) was a pivotal factor in the turn toward the position alluded to here.

17. Similar "third way" proposals have been offered by C. Ellis Nelson, *Where Faith Begins* (Richmond: John Knox, 1967) and by Westerhoff, *Will Our Children.*

18. See Richard M. Jones, *Fantasy and Feeling in Education* (New York: Harper, 1970).

19. See Moltmann, *Crucified God,* chs. 7 & 8; Juan Luis Segundo, *The Liberation of Theology* (Maryknoll, New York: Orbis Books, 1976); Paul Ricoeur, *Freud and Philosophy* (New Haven: Yale University Press, 1970); and Jürgen Habermas, *Knowledge and Human Interests* (Boston: Beacon, 1971).

20. See Claude Geffre and Gustavo Guttierez, eds., *The Mystical and Political Dimension of the Christian Faith* (New York: Herder and Herder, 1974). One of the central thrusts of Thomas Merton's writings in the last ten years of his life pushes powerfully in this direction. See Merton, *Conjectures of a Guilty Bystander* (Garden City, New York: Doubleday Image Books, 1968) and *Contemplation in a World of Action, ibid., 1973.* Two outstanding secondary sources on Merton are valuable in this connection: Henri J. M. Nouwen, *Pray to Live* (Notre Dame, Indiana: Fides/Claretian, 1972) and James T. Baker, *Thomas Merton Social Critic* (Lexington: University Press of Kentucky, 1971).

21. James Cone's theological project, especially his most recent book, *The God of the Oppressed* (New York: Seabury, 1975) is a powerful corrective in this regard for white minority elites in the U.S. and Europe.

22. The research on and theory of moral development generated by Lawrence Kohlberg and his associates is highly pertinent here. For a discussion of moral development, including attention to the role in it of widening social perspective-taking, see Kohlberg, "Moral Stage and Moralization" *Moral Development and Behavior,* Thomas Lickona, ed. (New York: Holt, Rhinehart & Winston, 1976). See also Fowler, *et al., Life Maps.*

23. Segundo, in *Liberation of Theology,* is particularly convincing on this point in his discussion of the "hermeneutical circle." See also Jose Miguez Bonino, *Christians and Marxists* (Grand Rapids; Eerdmans, 1976).

24. See references to my writings in note 12. *Life Maps* (1978) is the most comprehensive overview available at present. A major statement on faith development theory and research is underway at this writing.

Christian Hope and the Black Experience—*Noel L. Erskine*

1. Cf. John S. Mbiti, "Eschatology," in Kwesi Dickson and Paul Ellingworth, eds., *Biblical Revelation and African Beliefs* (Woking, Surrey Lutterworth, 1969), pp. 159–184.

2. James H. Cone, *The Spirituals and the Blues* (New York: Seabury, 1972), p. 90.

3. Harold A. Carter, *The Prayer Tradition of Black People* (Valley Forge, Pa.: Judson Press, 1976), p. 29.

4. Cone, *Spirituals and Blues,* p. 51.

5. Cited by H. S. Klein, *Slavery in the Americas,* (University of Chicago Press, 1967), pp. 113–14.

6. Klein, *Slavery in the Americas,* pp. 114–15.

7. Bryan Edwards, *The History: Civil and Commercial of the British Colonies in the West Indies,* Vol. 2 (London: printed for J. Stockdale, 1793–1801), pp. 38–39.

8. Klein, *Slavery in America,* p. 120.

9. H. Shelton Smith, *In His Image, But . . .* (Durham: Duke University Press, 1972), p. 13.

10. *Ibid.,* p. 12.

11. Wesley M. Gewehr, *The Great Awakening in Virginia, 1740–1790* (Durham: Duke University Press, 1930), p. 236.

12. *Ibid.,* p. 237.

13. *Ibid.,* pp. 236–37.

14. *Ibid.,* p. 239.

15. Klein, *Slavery in America,* p. 121.

16. *Ibid.,* p. 125.

17. Gerald Francis de Jong, "The Dutch Reformed Church and Negro Slavery in Colonial America," *Church History* 40, (March 1971), pp. 423–36.

18. Lawrence Jones, "Black Churches in Historical Perspective," *Christianity and Crisis,* (November, 1970), p. 227.

19. Gayraud S. Wilmore, *Black Religion and Black Radicalism* (Garden City, New York: Doubleday, 1972), p. 42.

20. Lovell, *Black Song,* p. 229.

21. Cone, *Spirituals and Blues,* p. 94.

22. See P. Gates, "George Liele," *The Chronicle* (1943), p. 124. See also Wilmore, *Black Religion and Radicalism,* pp. 106–07.

23. E. Franklin Fraser, *The Negro Church in America* (New York: Schocken Books, 1974), p. 30.

24. Wilmore, *Black Religion and Radicalism,* pp. 107, 108.

25. *Ibid.,* pp. 79–100.

26. Cf. *Religion, Revolution and the Future,* pp. 40 f., 129 ff.; *Crucified God,* pp. 330 f.; *Experiment Hope,* pp. 131–157; *Church in the Power of the Spirit,* pp. 182 f.; *Die Zukunft der Schöpfung,* pp. 117 ff.

27. Cf. "Warum Schwarze Theologie?" a special issue of *Evangelische Theologie* 34 (January 1974).

28. James H. Cone, *A Black Theology of Liberation* (Philadelphia: Lippincott, 1970), p. 245.

29. Major Jones, *Black Awareness: A Theology of Hope* (Nashville: Abingdon, 1971), p. 137.

30. Cf. Segundo, *Liberation of Theology,* and Rubem A. Alves, *A Theology of Human Hope* (New York: Corpus Books, 1969).

31. Jose Miguez Bonino, *Doing Theology in a Revolutionary Situation* (Philadelphia: Fortress, 1975), p. 149.

32. Moltmann, *Church in the Power of the Spirit,* p. 197.

33. Jürgen Moltmann, *The Passion for Life* (Philadelphia: Fortress, 1978), p. 102.